Between Two Worlds

Between Two Worlds

The Realm of Physical Phenomena

Allyson Walsh

Allyson Walsh
and Adele Nichols

To order additional copies of this book, contact:
Xlibris Corporation
1-888-795-4274
www.Xlibris.com
Orders@Xlibris.com

66093

Contents

Acknowledgements

Adele and I wish to thank Allen Gross for his cooperation and the use of his pictures in the section of this book on Spirit emanations, or 'orbs,' as they are called. We feel indebted to Steve and Tina McNaughton, for the use of their wonderful Chestnut Hall Bed and Breakfast in New Oxford, Pennsylvania, and for being instrumental in the ghost hunting expedition in 2007 of the Cashtown Inn near Gettysburg, Pennsylvania. We thank Emily Grace Freed for the use of her pictures from our stay at the Cashtown Inn, and Barbara Roberts and Barbara Menenghini for sharing their orb photographs. Thanks to M.J. Glagola for the 'White Ghost' photographs. We are grateful to Gladis Stroehme and Evelyn Carr (now in the Summerland), and Hoyt Robinette of Camp Chesterfield Spiritualist Camp in Chesterfield, Indiana for their wonderful ability in the development of the card and silk precipitations we have received. We send you blessings of abundance.

I also wish to thank my best friend, Stacey Sprenkle, now an angel on the 'other side,' for her assistance in getting this book in the 'right hands' for success, and for her overall help with the 'work.' Both of us miss you so very much.

Allyson and Adele

Prologue

Awakening to the Psychic Sense

Readers will readily agree if something paranormal happens to you or your family, you want to know what is going on! Many clients come to see us asking if what they experience is 'real.' I dare ask, "What is reality?" The recent movie, "What the Bleep Do We Know?" states that quantum physicists question 'reality.' Yogis and sages have been telling us for hundreds of years that our reality is an illusion. Young and old, people come to tell us what they see, hear, and experience. When our clients ask what it all is about, mostly we tell them nothing is wrong, that it is loved ones or spirit guides on the 'other side' trying to get in touch with them. Everyone wants to know they are not going crazy, or taking leave of their senses—and who else can they go to, but someone who challenges society to declare they are 'different? Perhaps 'enlightened' is a better descriptive.

Examples of incidents with our clients range from balls of light, ectoplasm, to ghosts of varying density appearing in photography. Flashes of light in the peripheral vision. Lights unexpectedly blinking, winking, or turning on and off take place. Clients experience feelings of hot or cold spots in rooms, smelling aromas such as perfume or smoke, and seeing everything from unexplained shadows to fully developed, materialized ghosts and angels. People speak of experiences ranging from ringing in the ears, ringing of telephones with no one on the other end, and objects of all kinds apporting, moving, appearing in their possession!

In fact, Allyson and I realize that as long as we have worked in the public, more and more people are coming forward with their experiences. Is this because societal standards and norms are once again allowing for a wave of spiritual enlightenment, such as that which occurred in the nineteenth century? Emmanuel Swedenborg and Andrew Jackson Davis were two early, courageous pioneers known for their understanding of the spirit realms. Davis predicted the coming of Spiritualism in his *Principles of Nature*, published in 1847, where he says, "It is a truth that spirits commune with one another while one is in the body and the other in the higher spheres—and this, too, when the person in the body is unconscious of the influx, and hence cannot be convinced of the fact; and this truth will ere long present itself in the form of a living demonstration. And the world will delight with the ushering-in of that era when the interiors of men will be opened, and the spiritual communication will be established . . . ." The first nationally known mediums, 'The Fox Sisters,' seized public fame and notoriety; it all began with them in Hydesville, New York, March 1847. They claimed to understand 'spirit rappings' as communication from the dead. Spiritualism was thus born and spanned an era of interest until it faded from larger popularity by the 1930s. Not to say there were no great mediums thereafter, there were, but the flower of spiritualism lasted approximately eight decades. It is possible that 'spirit interest' comes in movements? Is it possible the ocean of spirit is stirring like a tsunami once again?

Allyson and I believe this new wave of 'spirit interest' began gently rolling into the shore of mankind's consciousness in the 1980s, receded slightly in the 1990s, only to see the 'tsunami' sliding in once more to mass consciousness again in the new millennium, the twenty-first century. Great psychic mediums such as Gladis Stroehme, Reed Brown, and Hoyt Robinette, have helped shaped our work with their patience and wisdom. Pioneering psychic mediums such as Rosemary Altea, George Anderson, James Van Praagh, Sylvia Browne, and John Edward seen on television have helped create the tsunami-like interest in communication from the dead, as well as such movies in the media like *Ghost*, and *The Sixth Sense*. Rosemary Altea had to endure fearful audiences such as the one on Oprah Winfrey's show in the early 1980s. The opposite has now occurred with the premiere of the telecasts, *Crossing Over with John Edward, Beyond with James Van Praagh, The Ghost Whisperer, Paranormal State,* and *The Medium*. Television is now allowing for education and inspiration on the subject of transition and beyond, rather than simple sensationalism.

Where the psychic few have come into public view, now a larger phenomena is occurring. Many people from all walks of life are coming forward, telling us their narratives—accounts of experiences such as conversations with deceased loved ones or angels, and demonstrations of physical phenomena involving the supernatural world. Gone is the fear of reprisal; in its place a hunger for a sense of connectedness with others, including that of mystical experiences. Orthodox religions fall short of their original intention of offering structures for understanding, upliftment, and individual spiritual growth. Most often, people leave denominations because of the guilt/fear focus, or rigid faith systems that leave people feeling empty and unsupported in compassion. Exposure of religious corruption involving greed and sexual deviation amongst the priesthoods and evangelists has led the masses to soul-search and broaden their belief systems. As succinctly stated by Drs. Martha J. Barham and James T. Greene in their book, *The Silver Cord: Lifeline to the Unobstructed*, the western orthodox church has factionalized so in its divisiveness that it has become a 'means unto itself' rather than a 'means whereby." The spiritual search has led to a new maturity—to find God within! All who read this book will see what came naturally for us twofold as twins.

"God may for good and wise purposes, have separated the world of spirits from ours and communication was not granted except for cogent reasons, among those which mere curiosity should not be counted," stated Arthur Conan Doyle, in his work, *The History of Spiritualism*. However, by opening one's mind, welcoming the Universal Force, magnifying optimal idealism, and allowing virtues such as patience and generosity to unfold, ignites a hundredfold, if not indeed thousands of adventures with spirit, for all who are willing to take a leap of faith. Being skeptical, people want confirmation of their own psychic experiences, and need validation that these accounts are real. This book is devoted to: helping people understand their own inward quest; finding their level of experience; and helping them to 'fine-tune' their development. Here within these pages follow veridical accounts that spirit has demonstrated for Allyson and me, involving clairsentience, clairvoyance, clairaudience, and physical phenomena. Also included in several chapters of this book are narratives from clients which may help readers to recognize and expand their own abilities.

Allyson Walsh and Adele Nichols

Wake Now My Senses

Music: Traditional Irish/Slane—"Be Thou My Vision"
Lyrics by Thomas J. S. Mickelson, 1936-

Wake, now, my senses and hear the earth call,
Feel the deep power of being in all;
Keep, with the web of creation your vow,
Giving, receiving, as love shows us how.

Wake, now, my reason, reach out to the new;
Join with each pilgrim who quests for the true;
Honor the beauty and wisdom of time;
Suffer thy limit, and praise the sublime.

Wake, now, compassion, give heed to the cry;
Voices of suffering fill the wide sky;
Take as your neighbor both stranger and friend,
Praying and striving their hardship to end.

Wake, now, my conscience, with justice thy guide;
Join with all people whose rights are denied;
Take not for granted a privileged place;
God's love embraces the whole human race.

Wake, now, my vision of ministry clear;
Brighten my pathway with radiance here;
Mingle my calling with all who will share;
Work toward a planet transformed by our care.

Adele—'Mr. Greenjeans' and Two Little Girls

Our earliest and happiest memories of our working with spirit began when our parents bought a seven-acre farmette in Gambrills, Maryland, close by the state capital, Annapolis. The farm was elongated in its format; the formal cape-cod design stucco house was planted square in the middle of this plot of land with many gigantic oak and maple trees with hemlock. The front field ran parallel to Maple Road. Behind our home grew Mother's motley azalea gardens. Dad's workshop always smelled of new sawdust and oil. The playhouse that Dad built for us sat closest to the 'south forty,' where the peach and apple trees thrived. The backfield housed the two-car garage, our large vegetable garden, as well as the rabbit hutch. Our property extended at least an acre into the mysterious woods where our curiosity would take us now and then.

I recall several instances when imagination took full force of us as we played for hours with friends in the neighborhood or with just ourselves. Allyson and I have a younger sister who was just a baby at this time, and we had a next-door neighbor who was our gal pal. We played many imaginative games such as pretending to be 'horses' with our own stables and fields to run. Other times we played 'house,' using cardboard boxes or blankets draped over outdoor furniture. The playhouse was built because of our insistence to have a real 'cottage' after seeing the Walt Disney movie, *Sleeping Beauty*.

That large garden planted behind the garage was an acre or more, lined with apple and elm trees on one side. Behind the garden, the fenced-off woods led to the start of the Severn River tributary. Upon investigating the vegetable garden and woods, we encountered human and animal spirits and thought nothing of it to see these spirits in the 'back south forty.'

The spirits of animals fascinated us, as we saw them as mere shadows of blue-gray, but they could occasionally appear physically solid. I suppose we got used to seeing them after watching them appear and disappear before our eyes. Rabbits, foxes, and other wild creatures would come into focus as we played our garden game called 'Stone Soup.' We would gather old or rotten garden vegetables, find a suitable washpan or bucket, place vegetables along with a good-size stone in the broth—all of this in imitation of the fairy tales we heard as children. In these early years life was idyllic—there was a great deal to experience on our farm.

Perhaps it was because the days long past were slower and more carefree—minutes turned like hours and days likened to weeks to children of four and five years of age. All of the children in the neighborhood had the run of the community. Maple Road consisted of eight to ten properties; between them a series of well-worn paths used by the neighborhood children to visit one another. Some of the neighboring farms had an abundance of animal or human spirits that stayed with that property. Certain parts of the neighborhood had a particularly uncomfortable or foreboding 'feel,' as Allyson and I perceived this. Most of the farmettes were welcoming; we would play 'Hide and Seek,' also known as 'Commandos,' and 'Kick the Can,' crossing many boundaries with other kids to our great delight. The game of 'Kick the Can' entailed kicking a ball down a neighbor's hill, requiring one of us to go get the ball, and the others would hide. You were 'found,' if you were tagged with the ball, and the game started over again. Some of my best hiding spots which kept me from being found were given to me in my mind. I think that even then, at that early age, a protective spirit helped me in this way.

Most of the neighbors called children home through the ringing of a dinner bell, each with its own timbre and volume of ring. My siblings straggled in from whatever we were doing, and helped bring the dishes of steaming hot food and cutlery to the table. While eating, Allyson and I recounted our day by relating what we experienced. I remember many occasions our parents looking at each other, their eyes signaling unspoken words. We were young and naïve; our parents must have believed it was childish tales we invented to entertain the family. These childish tales unexpectedly changed when a dramatic event occurred that involved our favorite uncle-in-law, Marvin.

Marvin came into our lives when Allyson and I were about four to five years of age. He lived most of his life in the western Maryland area. When in his seventies, Marvin met our father's oldest sister, our Aunt Hazel, who eventually married him. I suppose Marvin and my father liked each other well enough prior to Marvin's marriage that he would visit and help out on our farm in the Gambrills area.

He moved into a tiny one-room cottage that was across the road from where we resided. Our Dad hired Marvin to perform various chores on our property, cutting grass in the large front field, working with tools in the tool shed, fixing automobiles, and working in the garden.

There wasn't anything that he couldn't work on; he was a handyman, a 'real jack of all trades.' Marvin worked with his hands since he was not an educated man. He drifted around from one job to another, using skills he picked up to good advantage. A hard drinker and smoker, his fingers were badly stained from tobacco. I recall him rolling his own cigarettes in the tool shed, carefully spilling the tobacco onto the white papers, licking the paper to hold the roll together. His voice was raspy and he coughed a great deal from the quantity of cigarettes he consumed. Despite his hard times, he knew how to joke and have a good laugh. His manner was gentle in regard to the children of our community. He had a soft heart for little girls, especially Allyson and me. My sister and I would sing along with the rock and roll songs playing on the radio in our dad's tool shed, with Marvin laughing at our attempts at dancing at such a tender age. Our parents were too busy managing a growing family and overseeing the farm to pay much attention. To have Marvin there with us, working and talking to my sister and me like we mattered, made quite an impression on us.

One characteristic of Marvin that my sister and I remember was the fact that he always wore farmer's blue jean overalls. He rarely wore anything else, and when a particular children's TV show called *Captain Kangaroo* featured a handyman wearing overalls, we started calling Marvin 'Mr. Greenjeans.' He seemed especially pleased that we gave him the nickname, and would answer us when we called him by his new identity.

Eventually, work slowed down on the farm, and Marvin returned to western Maryland, resuming life with Aunt Hazel. Time passed, and as we grew older, distant relatives reported to our parents that Marvin passed away in his sleep. Mother and Dad told us twins that Marvin went to 'heaven,' but our parents didn't give us many details about Marvin's passing. They must have felt that it wasn't important to tell us, being only five and three-quarter years of age.

Two weeks elapsed after Marvin's death. Allyson and I were playing in the back of the property by the garden, when an event occurred that would figure prominently in our later lives. We were playing games with each other one early Sunday afternoon, when Marvin stepped out from a shaw of hemlock trees that sidelined the garden next to our playhouse. He slowly lumbered towards us but stopped after we noticed him. He called our names, placing his hands in an upward motion to stop us from coming too close. Marvin spoke, saying, "I am sorry you cannot hug me, I haven't been 'home' yet." You must understand that he looked as real and solid-looking as any of us, only he had crossed over to the spirit world. He tenderly asked how we were doing, but told us our parents did not understand all that we could 'see.' We did not understand this! Marvin gently asked us to forward a communication to our mother and father for him (obviously something between adults). My sister and I were naturally excited about bringing this message back to our parents, which he presented to us as a memorization game. Once memorized, he told us to run back to the house and deliver the message once we arrived inside. As we raced towards the house, Allyson looked back to see our dear old friend turn away. As she watched, Marvin lost his earthly body as he slowly ambled into the hemlock trees.

Exuberant, we ran directly into the house where our mother was putting dinner on the table. Barely eating, we relayed the message to our parents several times, as they asked us to replay what had happened while we were outside. Of course they did not say much, but I do recall that both our parents gave each other incredulous looks of astonishment! Unfortunately, neither of us today recollect what Marvin passed along to our parents.

Before heading to the first grade in our community school, our parents pulled us aside and told Allyson and myself "not to say anything about we experience to our newfound friends and teachers at school." We nodded our heads, and went on to primary grade school without much thought about our special gifts.

Looking back now at this extraordinary time when Marvin spoke to us after his crossing, spirits of friends and relatives knew that Allyson and I had a unusual gift, given at an early age to bridge the gap 'between two worlds.'

Allyson—Accepting Our Difference

Individuals want to know how we developed as psychics and mediums, and since Adele has told her version of us learning at an early age, I wish that I could say that it happened all at once! But quite the contrary, the 'psychic sense' did not come with a bang all at once, rather, it would come and go involuntarily. As my sister Adele stated, we saw animals and humans in spirit form, and we accepted this without question. We naturally accepted that our 'Uncle Marvin' could appear to us in broad daylight, and talk to us on a Sunday afternoon out in the backfield of our parent's farmette near Annapolis, Maryland.

Living in such rural country, Adele and I sought our parent's acceptance of our 'gift.' We assumed, after all, that what we had was natural, but when Dad sat us down shortly before starting first grade to tell us "not to tell everyone what we see or hear, or people will think you are crazy" speech, Adele from that point on clammed up. It was difficult from that point onwards to talk to anyone about the things that I would experience, especially since now that Adele wanted to ignore it and be 'normal' like everyone else. Guidance concerning what I knew were paranormal events could not be found. Even 'Uncle Marvin' did not visit us again.

School years sped by for the both of us—it seems we were often teachers' pets, as Adele and I were artistic. From the moment our Mother put crayons in our hands, we both wanted to draw. Mother had to watch out for her hardcover books and walls in the house on more than one occasion! We spent many hours with just about any art medium, and we often spent extra-curricular time in school creating bulletin boards and projects. Adele and I were natural spellers; I won a national spelling contest in ninth grade given by a college. I loved school, and I am sure Adele did too, but we sometimes enjoyed pulling pranks on other students as well as teachers. When we entered high school, we were known to switch classes to see if we could fool instructors. Usually, we could keep it going for about ten minutes, and then the teachers would catch on. More than once, Adele and I were sent to principals' offices from grade-to-high school for our hi-jinks.

Adele and I learned to 'will' the ability away when we were about six or seven years of age. This happened, I think, due to the fact that we became distracted by what was in front of us—namely, school and friends. We spent many hours outside playing within a two-mile radius. I do not remember much involvement with television, and our mother didn't want to be distracted by us that much. So we climbed trees (higher than the boys), picked ripe, black cherries off of old Mr. Miller's property (with him chasing us off, waving his rifle wildly), played with neighborhood friends in games of 'kick the can,' hopscotch (the harder the better!), and hiding games. Pretend games were the best games—if we could drag our parents' clothes outside for costumes, the world became our stage. We girls were very involved in the neighborhood, and many of the adults on the streets where we lived knew us, but not as 'psychic twins.'

Of the two of us, I was slower to move into puberty, although I was the elder by five minutes. Adele was more interested in boys, while I was cautious. I remember playing commandos with the neighborhood boys after dark; I really saw myself as one of the gang. In my early teen years, Dad had to drag me in after 9PM from one of the commando games. Our parents decided then and there that we must start behaving like proper girls! Our parents made the decision when we were thirteen to start cotillion, a form of ballroom dancing taught in Annapolis, Maryland. We had to start wearing fancy dresses, stockings and shoes. This was alien for me, as a youngster—jeans and tee shirts were more my attire. I even wore long pants under school dresses in the wintertime. To this day, I still do not care for dresses.

We learned dance from a socialite couple, and eventually I was won over to enjoy dancing with boys. But I wasn't interested in boys to date. It wasn't until I met one boy at the cotillion that I was guardedly interested in, that I had my first wake-up call. Perry was cute, but I was tongue-tied and shy. I believe he took my shyness for being not interested, and decided to pursue my twin! It upset me for several years that Perry and Adele were an item, and that I was the outsider. As much as I tried to relate to boys in school, once they found out that I had the 'psychic sense,' they took off in the opposite direction!

Our parents raised us in the Methodist religious belief background. It was a comfortable setting for Adele and me when we were young; however, when I became sixteen years of age, I questioned authority. From an early period, I was a voracious reader, and found out there was a lot to be read 'between the lines' of the Bible. Perhaps because of my unusual nature, I saw life in series of images and symbols. Symbols stood out to me the way people see things on billboards. I was asked to leave Sunday school classes, because I plied too many questions to undereducated teachers. I was also asked to leave the junior choir I enjoyed so much, I think due to my soprano voice turning alto. All of this, including the difficulties of growing pains and socialization, made me feel ostracized by the very people I had grown to admire as a child and as a young adult. I was now seeing through different eyes.

It was when we turned sixteen that we both had a startling experience that I now relate. One cool night of September 1966 was to be a turning point for Adele and myself, although we didn't know it yet. Adele stayed home that evening ironing clothes for that school week. I attended the Sunday evening Methodist youth group at the church, and after it was over at 11PM, our friend Dianne asked if I could give her a ride home in my father's Volvo. I said yes, and off we went in the opposite direction from the church. Dianne didn't live far, just ten minutes away. After we said our good-byes, I headed back towards the church on Route 178. Perhaps it was five minutes later, that I had a startling 'waking' vision, which verily saved my life.

Driving home meant heading back towards the church, and home was less than a half-mile from there on Route 178. Millersville Road intersects Route 178, also known as General's Highway, right where the Methodist church resides. It was about 11:20PM and very dark. It was about three miles from the church crossroads, when all of a sudden I heard a man's voice from the backseat of the car I was driving! The voice loudly said, "Slow down!" and as it faded away, I saw in the windshield the scene I was to see a few minutes later in front of the church.

The windshield in front of the steering wheel wasn't there anymore. A vision of my car sliding into a small dark-red sedan full of people commenced, and I watched this, helpless, as the Volvo was headed to hit this vehicle. I knew that something was wrong with the brakes on my car, which I locked up trying to avoid hitting the sedan. The dark-red sedan ran the stop sign on their side of the crossroads. I could hear the brakes on my car squealing as the car slid inevitably into the red sedan. I could hear the four occupants laughing, as they sped into the crossroads. I anxiously remember shouting to myself, "Oh my God, oh my God!" praying that I don't hit this car, that they see me in time to move faster through the crossroads so we avoid each other. But they did not. The bumpers of both vehicles ended up 'hooking' each other, and while the red sedan moved through the intersection as though nothing happened, the Volvo spun several times as the brakes did not hold. I remember screaming for help. After several spins, the brakes finally caught and held, just before the car ran off the road into a culvert at the church crossroads. There is no shoulder on that area of road, to speak of. The brakes slammed the car into a stop, and without seatbelts, my head hit hard the windshield before I lost consciousness. I cannot say how long my unconsciousness lasted; no one must have come through the intersection, or stopped to see what transpired. My car was on the wrong side of the road, facing the Methodist church. I remember that the first thing I was aware of when I woke up was the stained-glass arched window in the church lit from inside, and that my hands gripped like steel on the steering wheel. I couldn't move them.

Gradually my vision focused on the backlit church stained-glass window. My ears surprised me to find myself talking to thin air! I heard myself say out loud, "But what we think is reality is totally different!" *Who was I talking to?* I looked at the passenger and back seats, thinking that someone stopped to help. There was no one. I stiffly moved my fingers from the steering wheel one-by-one, and got out of the car. I ached. My body, rigid as a board, moved in slow motion, and my head hurt terribly between the eyes. The shadowy road smelled dank, and my car was within an inch of falling into the culvert. "Saved by a voice," I hoarsely whispered, feeling cold. Managing to get the Volvo restarted, I drove the quarter mile back home, leaving the car outside, dreading to face my parents. I rang the backdoor bell, believing they locked it on purpose, since I didn't get home on time. Adele ran downstairs, eyes large and wringing her hands when she saw me, pale and drawn from my ordeal.

"Oh, I knew it! I knew it!" exclaimed Adele. "I knew something happened to you! When I was ironing, I felt something was going to happen to you, and I tried to tell our parents. I tried to get Dad to go down to the church, it felt so real!" Adele looked at me shivering from the shock, pulling me down into a chair. Adele yelled frantically upstairs to our parents to come, and I remember Dad looked at his car, then me. It turned out that both cars kissed each other; the Volvo ended up with a dark-red stripe on the front bumper. Frustrated by the lack of parental concern, Adele and I went upstairs to our bedroom, where our Mother came and listened to what occurred over the last quarter hour. I went to bed shortly, but I recall now something that our Mother did that week, which was contradictory to her later behavior—she went to the library and brought back a book by Jesse Stern entitled, *The Search for the Girl with Blue Eyes*. Mother also brought me a book titled, *There is a River*, about Edgar Cayce, the twentieth century's 'sleeping prophet.' I devoured both books, and wanted more. From that time forward, I spent many an hour looking for books at the local library to see if there were other individuals like Adele and myself.

High school thereafter was difficult; indeed, life itself was a hard reality. Powers such as clairsentience and clairvoyance became second nature to me. As a backlash to my abilities, my peers held great reluctance to accept me as one of their own. Brazen boys slyly asked me in the bleachers at Arundel High School who I thought would win basketball games. The attention was flattering until I came to realize they weren't interested in *me*, but for my abilities to call the games which they bet upon. I soon realized that I had to date boys from other grades, other schools out-of-county, and later, out of state. I felt terribly alone and ostracized. Boys didn't care about me deeply, which made it hard to relate to them. I spent much of high school studying hard to graduate, looking for ways to hide. I spent time incessantly outside at night talking to God, asking *why do I have this ability,* only to have others be afraid of it. As college drew near, I wanted more than anything to be normal, not known for an extraordinary talent.

Speaking to God one night under the wheeling stars finally brought an answer. I 'heard' a male voice in my head, whom I now know to be Barnabas, telling me to understand that I would be a teacher this lifetime. Even though I would marry, I would not have children. I recall sitting outside on one of the cold, grey concrete seats in the backyard, a light breeze wafting. I thought, "Well, that will be OK." Time enough to become a teacher. Who knew what the future would bring?

Allyson—Meeting an Angel

1981 was a year that I hope never to relive. I had separated from my first husband Bernie in November of that year because of his denial of his addiction to alcohol. In retrospect, I believe that he married me for something other than love. He courted me while he had a white-collar job working for Volkswagen of America. While it appeared that he was decent and sober, I suppose that I should have seen disaster coming when he announced two months before our marriage that he was fired from his job. Bernie was able to get a job running a marine repair shop for a large marine retail sales company in Deale, Maryland; however, it required our moving near his new office. His salary was one-third less than what he wanted. Hours after our wedding, we spent our honeymoon at the Maryland Inn where I was surprised that he could drink everyone within the vicinity under the table. I never dreamed that I would marry a deceptive drunk. We spent nine years with me trying to hold the marriage together. I took care of the house, yard, cooking, and running my own graphic production business. My husband Bernie drank Manhattans and beer as soon as he came home from a job he hated because the summer meant twelve-hour workdays. The winter offered Bernie the only time to weave dreams of what he wanted to become. I spent many hours in the first years of our marriage coaching him, encouraging him to pursue his dreams, but he preferred drinking to doing. By the ninth year of our marriage, we had no married couples as friends, and the only friends that we had were mostly single males who held no responsibility. Bernie and his friends spent countless hours after work and weekends out on their boats. I tried to fit into this picture the first three or four years of our marriage, but I saw how much denial I owned as well in this miserable relationship. I enabled his lifestyle, but I wanted more. By May of 1981 I gave an ultimatum to Bernie—either get help for his addiction or I would move out in six months. I belatedly felt bad for giving him the ultimatum on his birthday, but I was sick of holding our marriage together. I lost so much weight, that my family thought I was anorexic. I went from 135 pounds to 98 pounds in one year; all I could find were jeans in boys' sizes to wear. I was so stressed, that I threw away any pictures that I had of myself from that awful time.

When six months passed, Bernie got up one morning, and shook me awake. Groggily, I arose and found my wallet that he demanded I bring him. I sat on the bed as he took the credit cards from the wallet and cut them up, chuckling as if this was a huge joke. Bernie then announced that this was the day I should pack up my things and get out. It felt like lightning passed through my body; the hair on the nape of my neck was standing on end. I couldn't speak right away. It took everything within me to keep from wanting to run him through with a knife, but fear got the better of me, as he could be downright ugly mean. So I sat on the bed without emotion, even as he went downstairs and walked out of the house. I think I stayed there for about two hours before I called my Dad to ask him to come get what things I could easily move out of the house before Bernie got home. Inasmuch as my Dad never involved himself in my siblings' lives up to this point in time, he arrived with the family station wagon. Without a word about the crisis, my father helped me load up. Dad moved the larger items back home, and I moved in with a girlfriend in Annapolis until I knew what to do. I stayed for about two weeks, but ten days later at my friend's house I received a call from Bernie. He wanted me to meet his 'marriage counselor,' a psychotherapist who offered counseling for couples. I made it clear over the telephone that I was angry and not interested in coming back to the marriage, but I conceded that the marriage counselor needed to hear my side of the story. So I went for two sessions, one by myself, and the second with Bernie present.

We never did get back together. After the second meeting, the psychotherapist called me to tell me that I did the right thing, and that she was there to help Bernie with his problems. I moved up to Baltimore by the end of 1981 to live in an apartment, and for the first time in my life, I was alone.

The first three months in Baltimore was a shock to the system—I couldn't sleep for the background traffic noise. Shopping at the local food stores in the Pikesville area was a new experience, as I had never seen some of the kosher foods that were prominently displayed before this time. My mother made it clear in her few telephone calls to me how disappointed she was that I was divorcing, as I was the 'first in the family' to do this. After the last distressing telephone call, Mother didn't speak to me for a year, and Dad was silent as usual. I felt like I might as well have moved to the moon. I felt alienated, and bitterly alone.

March of 1982 was Adele's and my birthday, and I don't remember celebrating. All I could do was imagine the many ways one could commit suicide. I remember being in the bathtub with water all around me, with just my face out of the water. "It's not so hard to drown. Jeff (our brother) drowned when he was eighteen months old. It looks easy." I surmised. I grudgingly got out of the tub to dry off. My publishing clients needed me—that was all.

The following two weeks I was vaguely aware that physical phenomena was occurring in the apartment, but I didn't pay much attention. As far as I was concerned, I got up, took care of hygiene, cooked vegetarian (my adrenal system was so flat due to stress that I developed hypoglycemia), and worked over my drafting board producing magazine artwork. This was my dull, boring routine. But during all of this, balls of light would appear around the ceiling, unseen hands would stroke me, and even music played out loud one morning just as I was waking up. I thought I must have set a radio alarm clock in the kitchen, but when I sleepily arrived to turn it off, there was no alarm clock, no radio in the kitchen. The music died as I slowly woke up in disbelief.

Another day passes. I take a shower, and stand in front of the bathroom mirror putting on mascara, getting ready to work all day by myself, putting together a magazine. I was so good at production work, printers from Washington, DC to Baltimore 'cold-called,' wanting me to do production and post-production work. I didn't have to pound the pavement looking for work. As I swept the wand over my eyelashes, I felt a hand pull on my left elbow, forcing me to take two steps backwards out of the bathroom door. I don't know what enticed me to look to the apartment door, where the foyer and dining room was. Standing there was a very tall, radiant, white and gold being.

I stood in shock, unable to move, staring at this incredibly tall entity, whose head went through a nine-foot ceiling. My eyes traveled the length of him; his hair was shoulder-length, wavy, glowing with gold light. His face was fair with piercing, blue eyes. The body was elongated, El Greco-style, and from the crown to his knees his body looked opaque. Past the knees, however, the legs faded to nothing; there were virtually no feet. Gold energy crackled, emanated and held his bodily form together. There was a sense of a large, white egg-shaped aura, like a halo, that shone around the trunk and head. "A spirit," I assumed.

"No, I am not a spirit. I am neither male nor female, I am not of this Earth" spoke the entity. I don't know why I didn't react to this. The next thing I knew, I woke as if from a trance state in another part of the apartment, with what appeared to be smoke whirling, fading away. It disappeared, and I went straight away back to putting on mascara in the bathroom! As I put make-up on, I heard a voice, traveling in a 360-degree direction all around me.

"My name is Ariel, and I am here to protect you. Behind you is Joel." I could feel the warm presence of a man in spirit, less than my own height. "You need our help." With this, the voice stopped, and my body quaked with the realization that now I was hearing voices on top of visions! I couldn't help myself—I started crying, helpless to understand what was happening. I called June, a metaphysical teacher, who had taught me tarot divination; she was a friend (so I thought) and president of a local massage company. I tried to describe to her what I experienced, but she negated that I experienced anything. She didn't believe in ghosts, much less the spirit world. I called another woman I knew, Barbara, who was a locally-known channeler, and went to see her that day. Work would have to wait!

Barbara, in her deep state of trance, told me that there was indeed spirit involvement, as she stated there were 'two beings involved.' I never mentioned this to her. The information was helpful, but I still didn't know enough, or what to do with it.

I called a friend named Steve, whom I used to work with in Alexandria, Virginia, telling him what transpired. Steve was a photographer by trade, caught up with a deep interest in the paranormal. Steve himself had been studied at a young age at Duke University for his ability to 'astral travel.' Strangely, while I was married to Bernie during my work stint with Steve, I was not involved metaphysically until the last two years of our marriage. Steve offered to arrange my meeting a psychic in his building where he lived, and I asked him not to tell the psychic anything until I saw her. I was scared of meeting her, because I heard she was good. I understand now why people react to me in that way.

The psychic asked me to sit in the room with her, where she went into a trance state with her eyes wide open. She seemed frozen in her chair, until minutes later she told me in a low voice, "There are two people in the room with us; they are from the spirit world. One is a man in spirit with a name that starts with a 'J,' and the other just flits around the room. I don't believe he is a spirit, I think this one is an angel. He calls himself an angel, a 'throne angel' named Ariel. He is here to protect you. You are going to experience a bad year, but it will be all right in the end. Don't worry." I was sitting in a chair right next to the door, which was intentional, because I did not want to hear bad news. I didn't know whether to get up or stay, so I stayed. I must have looked worried, I am sure, because this psychic, whose name I cannot remember, looked at me sympathetically and said, "Don't worry, it appears you will be growing immensely this year and the next. Stay close to Steve, your friend." I left shortly, to join Steve downstairs in the apartment house, and told him what happened. I know this sounds crazy, but I was in denial, and had a hard time connecting with all of this. I think Steve was miffed with me, and he didn't take my calls too long thereafter. I was more concerned with having a 'pity-party' concerning my state of affairs, rather than be interested in the spirit phenomena. It took me a few months to work on healing.

I took a temporary roommate to live with me that summer, to help with expenses. Wanda was training for a job with the above-mentioned massage company that signed a contract to provide massage therapists with Downtown Athletic Club, a large fitness company in Baltimore. She was very busy working and studying to be certified to work for this health company. I told her several times that I had an uneasy feeling that something was going to go wrong with this deal. Wanda ignored me, and I tried to ignore the dreams that increased in intensity concerning Wanda and the massage company. I usually wrote-off dreams because they never seemed to make much sense, but finally in September, I woke up screaming after three nights of nightmares that indicated this massage company losing the contract. I got out of bed, and shouted out loud, "OK! If I am supposed to say something to the president of this company, you spirits had better send me a sign!" I was not at all happy to be the deliverer of bad news to June, the president of the massage company, as she was not open to many metaphysical ideas, even if she was the one that taught me the tarot.

I unhappily received my sign later that day, and dutifully drove to the massage company to share my information about the lost contract. June stared at me like I was crazy once I delivered the dream message. She went over to a table and held up the signed contract. "Looks like you are wrong, Allyson," she coldly replied. I silently shook my head, feeling it was time to leave. I went straight home, pulled pots and pans out for dinner, when Wanda walked in the door. Wanda seemed frustrated, venting about Richard, the instructor for the company. She didn't believe me when I insisted that the contract would not hold. Matter-of-factly, I exclaimed, "I tell you, the massage company won't be around too long. Tell June yourself." I went back to cooking, but something unfortunate pulled at me to look at the calendar on the wall—one date in September appeared as if it were written in red fire! I caught Wanda's attention, pointing to the month, and enigmatically stated, "Look, Wanda, do you see that date? The number '18' is all red; that will be *the day* your company fails to deliver its contract with Downtown Athletic Club." Wanda looked at me, shocked, but didn't ask me to elaborate on what I meant. I think Wanda knew that her company was in trouble. Ironically, I concluded by saying, "I think that your massage company is about to lose everything. You might as well start packing—the company will be closing by the end of the year." The agreement *was* broken on September 18, the date I pointed out to Wanda. Many of the trainees ended up suing both companies in a class-action suit, but Wanda lost interest in working in Baltimore. She packed up and went back to New Jersey. June, the massage company president, was furious about the loss of revenue. I had a devil-of-a-time collecting money on advertising that I placed for her company, and for some reason, she indirectly blamed me for the lost contract! Eventually I hired a collection lawyer, who pressured the massage company into paying me. The massage company broke its lease and dismantled by the end of 1982. Seven months later, June contacted me, inviting me to become an apprentice to her, and wanted to meet for a Chinese dinner close to my home. I cautiously agreed to get together, needing to see where this was going. Where June had once been a friend, now she was into power and manipulation. She wanted all of her apprentices to live in a communal house, give over their fortunes and belongings to be shared equally, yet have but minion status. She wanted to be objectified as a guru, however, it turned out to be a farce—she thrived on power over less confident individuals. In visiting her commune, I could readily see how terrified her student apprentices were of her. I vowed no more to be associated with her. Soon enough, June disappeared, not to be heard from since. Sadly, June was a 'legend in her own mind,' desiring to control others, using divination as her means of manipulation. A great lesson was learned through observation of how some people want power for its own sake, and I saw how power corrupts its owners. As stated in the Bible, 'And with what measure ye mete, it shall be measured to you again.' (Matthew 7:2) Justice will be served on all who do not live a balanced life through a balanced mind. Power must be used for good, and used in service to others.

Shortly after this, the spirit Joel left me for good (as far as I know). Ariel, the 'throne angel,' has consistently added his name to the card precipitations I receive through the mediumship of Hoyt Robinette, Gladis Stroehme, Evelyn Carr, and others—all of whom I wasn't to meet until almost a decade later. The curious thing is that I *am* curious—I wanted to know more about this angel Ariel. I spent time looking in libraries, not coming across much until I found a book called *The Dictionary of Angels*. In it, 'Ariel' is described as meaning 'Lion of God,' and 'Earth's great Lord,' and that Jewish mystics used Ariel as a poetic name for the city of Jerusalem. In the Bible the name denotes, variously, 'a man, a city, and an altar' (Isaiah 29). Sayce, author of *Athenaeum*, October 1886, wrote that he sees a connection between Ariel and the arelim (erelim), the valiant ones spoken of in Isaiah 33:7, an order of angels equated with the order of thrones. In occult readings Ariel is the 'third archon of the winds.' Mention is made of Ariel as 'an angel who assists Raphael in the cure of disease.' Well, I was floored. I couldn't stop thinking of this for months. To think that an angel wants to protect little mortal me! To complicate matters more, Barnabas, my Master Guide, lived in Jerusalem two thousand years ago, and I wondered how all of this fit into the picture.

Upon reflection years later, I believe Ariel, if so described as a 'throne angel,' must work to help his or her charges in the sense of wielding justice in the name of righteousness. Such a lesson was learned by me concerning the usage of knowledge and power, and I have since become a proponent of standing up for the underdogs of this world, especially when 'might believes it makes right.' Those people that hold sway to this belief find that power for its own sake, at the end of all things, will indeed corrupt entirely—as have entire empires and nations become as dust on the four winds.

"Partridge in a Pear Tree" card precipitation,
through the mediumship of Reverend Evelyn Carr, now deceased.

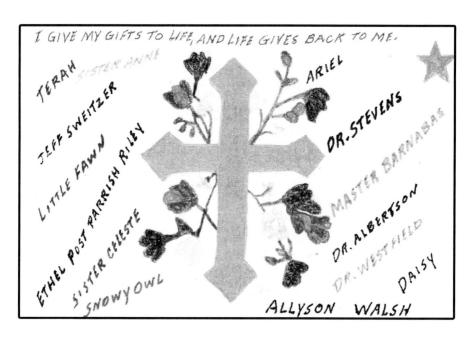

"Easter" card precipitation,
through the mediumship of Reverend Evelyn Carr, now deceased.

Allyson—The Look of Death

After the divorce from my first husband Bernie, I moved to Baltimore in December 1981 to work closely with the aforementioned company involved in massage and stress management. The company was relatively new to the area, like me. I was still involved with magazine production, but advertising was a refreshing diversion for me. Since I knew the president of the company, I was asked to put together their advertising program. It worked out well for them.

In the fall of 1983 this company would disband from poor management (as described in the chapter, 'Meeting an Angel'). I spent hours, days, and weeks working over my drafting board. I rarely expended time investigating my new surroundings. I admit that I spent an inordinate amount of time in my apartment, working, eating, listening to music, or sleeping. My life turned upside down since my divorce up to this time. Before I was to meet my second husband, it seems spirit found it imperative to show me new things.

I presume that if one must work with spirit, then it would be normal for a medium-in-training to have the ability to see impending death. Not that the training conducted by Barnabas, Dr. Albertson, or Little Fawn (an early joy guide I was to know a little by 1981, who even now, remains an enigma) was in so many words broadcast into my mind. Rather, many of my lessons were taught in extraordinary ways. Death was about to be shown to me in the most unusual circumstances.

I remember the date of October 22, 1983 like it was yesterday. I was working in my apartment den, which I converted into an efficient office. It was quite late; I was still working over the drafting board, putting together pages for a trade magazine. The television blared as a noisy background to keep me from thinking too much about my loneliness. Eventually, I stretched my muscles, lumbering past the television, hoping to get something from the kitchen to nibble. I glanced at the eleven o'clock news; I had the NBC network on, noticing anchorwoman Jessica Savitch was speaking. There was something odd about her this evening.

I returned from the kitchen with pretzels and settled on the couch to watch Jessica relay the nightly news. It slowly dawned upon me that a faint, black 'cloud' was visible around her as she sat at the news desk. I was intrigued—I had never seen a black aura before. A white aura around a specific minister was first viewed when I sat in church in my early teens, but a black aura? This dark emanation moved slightly as Jessica moved in her chair. My hair stood up, a chill running throughout goose-pimpling my arms. I blurted out, "She will be dead soon!" I was stunned by my own remark, and looked around the room as if someone else could hear me. When was she to die? I didn't know how to react to this. Cognizant that I was tired, I turned the television off when the news finished. I retired to bed, and fell asleep soundly.

The next morning presented my regular routine of dressing, eating, and resuming my work at the drafting board. I recall turning on the television for background chatter. At some point I became aware that a newsman was talking about the untimely drowning death of Jessica Savitch overnight. I couldn't believe my ears! I sprang up from the drafting board to become glued to the TV—I needed to hear what had happened to her. Unfortunately, not many details concerning her death were forthcoming that morning, but later that evening it was known that she had had dinner with Martin Fischbein in New Hope, Pennsylvania. Both left the restaurant in a downpour of rain. He mistakenly drove down a towpath that led to the Delaware Canal. The couple drowned in the car, along with Jessica's dog. News anchors on different networks repeated similar facts, including the fact that Jessica Savitch, being one of the first female anchorwomen, opened the field for women broadcasters.

What was I to make of the visual demonstration that spirit had me see? I wasn't sure of what to make of it, nor what to do with it. To tell you the truth, it scared me. I shuddered to know the truth of Jessica's passing. If I had been Catholic, I would have 'crossed' myself at that moment. The hard realization of the 'look of death' did not sit too well with me then, nor does it now.

It is painful to know someone is about to die. I have had to come to terms with this knowledge, just as I have had to with other lessons from Spirit. I have seen other individuals in casual settings, where I was to learn from the dark gray cloud around their head that they were sick. One man that I was forced to sit next to one day in the studio audience of Baltimore WJZ Channel 13's talk show, *People Are Talking*, gave me an uncomfortable feeling. I could see dark gray lines and streaks around his body, and I felt sick. The man next to me managed to commandeer a microphone, to tell the experts on the show that he had AIDs! No wonder I knew something was wrong!

Lastly, there is another 'look of death' that has since been introduced to me. I have mentioned elsewhere in the book that Adele and I had to contend with our mother's long-suffering illness due to Parkinson's disease. Mom refused to be fed through a tube in her gut after she had a heart attack onset with pneumonia. She had several close calls from complications of pneumonia (which is often the way victims of Parkinson's pass), due to aspiration of food into the lungs, setting up infection. Doctors found it hard to believe that she would survive the lung infections, but the third time it happened, which was in December 2003, the pneumonia weakened her to such an extent, that even though she would survive once more, it became clear to me that she was going soon. I took Dad to see Mom in the hospital during that last pneumonia bout. With antibiotics pumped into her intravenously, and an oxygen mask over her face, her eyes belied what she herself could not say. Even if she could have talked, which she could not at this advanced, final stage of Parkinson's, *her eyes* told me that she was 'ready' to go. I saw her soul speak the language of emotion— words did not have to be spoken. Fighting back tears, I haltingly gave Dad the news in the car when we left the hospital, that Mom would probably be released back to Heritage Harbor Rehabilitation Center by the end of the week, but she would be back again for another reason. With the help of Dr. Albertson, my physician guide, I knew, too, that she would leave this world by the end of January. I told Dad so, and in the following days I relayed the news as well to my siblings.

Yes, the doctors released her after the bout with pneumonia to the rehab center, only for her to be back in the hospital four days later from another infection. The doctors at the rehab center saw that she was going downhill, and prepared the family by telling us that they, too, felt that she would die in just weeks. A confirmation. Again, Mom was released back to the rehab center before the New Year. Dad's birthday was celebrated January 20, and Mom passed away two days later, suddenly, from aspirated food in her lungs. She most likely developed a pulmonary embolism or a clot in the lungs; within two minutes, she was dead.

There has since been just a sprinkling of people sitting in my office, where I have had this foreknowledge of their death. I do not like knowing about impending death, but it *is* the opposite of life and a fact. I will never tell a client sitting in an individual session or group that they are about to die if I possess the information. I believe Dr. Albertson, my spirit chemist, and his team of physicians, want *me* to know, but I cannot bring myself to tell this to someone—it is beyond good reason to do that. And it is not appropriate! What I will do is caution the client to pay close attention to their health and do all they can to maintain it. Psychics and mediums 'cross the line' when the health foreknowledge is used to manipulate and control unwitting people. I have heard horror stories from clients who have been misguided by exploitive fortunetellers.

Dr. Albertson's portrait and name on a card precipitation through the mediumship of Reverend Hoyt Robinette. He was an English eye doctor, who died in the pandemic Spanish influenza of 1917-18.

In the chapter titled 'More Signs and Wonders,' I speak of my closest friend Stacey, whom I had an uneasy feeling about for months before I finally said something about her health to her in December of 1999. Warned by a mutual medium friend several years before that Stacey might develop cancer, she and I were shocked to hear that message (another piece of bad news I won't deliver to clients). By late 1998, Stacey was told by her doctors that she was presenting with pre-cancerous cells in her pap smears, and that she would need to be tested twice a year. She had been to her OB/GYN in November 1999 for a clinical visit, received a clean bill of health, but by New Years Eve 2000 at my home in Annapolis, she discovered a lump in one of her breasts. It turned out to be 'stage 2 cancer,' which means it grew exceedingly fast! So, you see, even my friends are not immune from hearing about their state of health, if Dr. Albertson and his team of specialists inform me.

I will never, *ever*, tell someone that they are dying, even if they themselves present the information that *they* know they *are*. If I know that an older member of a client's family is passing soon, then I will warn the client that a member may leave of their own accord, and to ready themselves to be there for that individual, so that there will be no regrets afterwards. Because death itself is a fact of life, Adele and I have had discussions about how to 'forewarn with foreknowledge,' and only then if the spirit doctors think it is OK. Every individual case is acknowledged by spirit before anything is revealed. It is a tightrope difficult to traverse.

An interesting case of forewarning and foreknowledge came to my attention in 1998, when a woman called to make an appointment to see me. Upon her arrival, it became clear that she was hesitant to tell me about a special 'gift' that she recently acquired. It turned out Mimi really didn't want a reading; she wanted to confess that she did not know what to do with recurrent dreams that presented disasters and imminent death. I am fascinated by this ability, but Mimi clearly was not! She told me when Spirit let her know when a commercial airplane was to crash, she would have two or three weeks of the same dream. Mimi would even see the airplane occasionally as if she was on the tarmack, observing the plane on the ground or in the air. She could often tell which airline the plane belonged to by means of their logos, as well as flight numbers. After several weeks of nightmares, she would wake to hear of the exact plane go down. After several devastating episodes, she decided she needed to tell someone—who better than to tell another psychic?

I asked Mimi if she ever considered contacting the Federal Aviation Administration. She looked at me with horror. "Are you crazy, they will want to haul me into a room somewhere, and interrogate me for weeks." The problem of hijackers and terrorists, especially after September 11, 2001—I immediately saw her point. But I also realized that if Mimi truly saw the 'future' of those airplanes, how could she not want to do something to save countless lives? We went around on this at several meetings together. She was afraid to lose what normalcy she had in her life.

After more months passed, with more dreams with catastrophes ensuing, I petitioned Mimi once more to do something, but she was adamant she would not. I finally told her, that in all decency, I would take the matter into my own hands and call the FAA in Washington, D.C. to see if there was an office that would take calls from psychics about such things. I made several calls, and I was connected to an office at Reagan International Airport. The fellow was probably in his mid-forties, and was clearly not interested in hearing about this! He claimed that he didn't know of an office affiliated with the FAA who took such reports, but would I like to talk to someone at the Baltimore-Washington airport? I felt the guy was trying to blow me off, and I gave up trying. I relayed to Mimi of the aborted attempt with the FAA. A good try, but it didn't go anywhere. If anyone does know how and where to contact someone at the FAA, let me know.

Mimi ultimately willed the ability away after she saw John F. Kennedy, Jr.'s airplane go down. The dreams of John's imminent death lasted for several weeks before it occurred. The only thing that was different was that Mimi saw John's earlier airplane crash, not the one he was in. The thing is, it did happen, but Mimi had all she could take of the 'death dreams.' I can't say that I blame her. Psychics who see death, dream about death, or see future catastrophes need a great deal of care. I feel for Mimi and others that have that ability. I bless them and know that this kind of gift may be right for them. It takes a strong person to deal with death, and it helps to have a psychic connection of what to expect on the 'other side.'

Allyson—Barnabas

Earlier in this book I described my first contact with a 'male voice' coming from the backseat of my Dad's Volvo and the near-fatal car accident that I was rescued from by this same spirit. After this episode, I had many contacts from this same spirit individual, mainly by hearing his voice in my head. I was disconcerted at first when he came through when I least expected it, but it was clear that Barnabas was here for my awakening from a long sleep. Clearly he was here to teach me things not taught in physical schools, as spiritual values and morals were high on his list. Barnabas was around to tell me that 'integrity' was large on this list; it made me feel that I might not have had much in that department in the past, such as my past lives. Who knows?

During the period when I despaired over the lack of dating my male peers in high school, in my meditations while sitting outside under the stars I remember Barnabas describing himself when he lived in some of his last incarnations. Which brought up the concept for me about reincarnation. The book by Jess Stern, *The Search for the Girl With the Blue Eyes*, was the first time I had heard about reincarnation, but now this man, Barnabas, described to me what a couple of his lives had been. He adroitly admitted that he was the Barnabas of the Biblical period, uncle to Mark or Marcus, and apostle of Jesus. He made his living as a merchant, traveling often to trade and pass on news to different communities. After the crucifixion, he often traveled with Paul to distant lands, sometimes bringing Mark on these excursions.

His very last life was in southeast Ireland, in the fourteenth century. He eked out a living on a feudal manor near the Barrow River close to Kildare, working to support a sickly wife with six children. Three of the last would die before they reached puberty. I found out that I, Allyson, was the last-born child, bound to die when I was four years of age. Life was incredibly hard then, as famine and plague took its toll on everyone. Barnabas, along with other Irish dreamers, hoped to find another land west, and set out aboard an acquired ship. The dream was not to be—the ship foundered at sea before it reached western territories. He ended his description by stating that in his demise by drowning, he experienced his full enlightenment by this last transpiration of his met karma. He needed no longer incarnate on physical worlds!

I recall I was in my bedroom that I shared with my twin sister Adele one evening after the near-accident. I was studying and doing homework, when I heard Barnabas' voice in my head. I was reaching a point of familiarity with him in that I would sometimes speak out loud to him (if I was alone). I remember saying hello to him, and he replied, "Greetings, lass. I am here as your Master Guide. This one will teach you what is necessary to understand what God is."

"What is a Master Guide?" I silently asked, intrigued. Barnabas quietly said, "A Master Guide is one who is the leader of all the guides that work with and for you. I am Barnabas, and that is what you shall call me, but there have been others that have called me Saint Barnabas, for I lived during those times when the Christ walked on earth." I was amazed.

"Why do I have you, the one they call Saint Barnabas? How do I 'rate' having a saint?" I asked this question in a cantankerous manner.

"You do not 'rate' having a saint. Being called a saint on this planet called Terra is a by-product of having lived an extraordinary life in ordinary time. The people called the 'Catholics' of the Christian religious experience deem sainthood important, and it has been thus for over a thousand of these earth years. Not that sainthood is important to me—it is just a title—that is all. A label. A form of identification. I am just who I am, a spark of God. You, too, are a spark of God, who needs to remember why she is here. It is to learn about your Self, and that is why I am here."

I am in awe. I ask, "Does everyone have a saint for a Master Guide?" Barnabas replied, "No, the Master Guide chooses one or many, many living individuals on your Terra (Earth) and on other worlds to supervise, but the Master Guide does not tell you what to do. There is, in most cases, a still, quiet voice that impinges one's innermost mind to guide one along one's path. We cannot will anyone to do anything. There may be times that a Master Guide will incarnate with a living student in order to help him or her to overcome obstacles to growth, but in most cases, the Master Guide needs not incarnate anymore, and help can be facilitated in a larger capacity this way."

Barnabas then proceeded to tell me, "I will be with you this lifetime in order to help you move forward in your spiritual development. But in knowing who I am, you must be silent about this with many of those you know in the living until time comes when others are able to understand what this is about. I am a teacher, and will teach you concepts that you were able to just begin to grasp when you were forced to leave your Sunday school classes. I will teach you spiritual laws about virtues needed to live on Terra. Commandments. Laws. Rules of what to do and not to do. This will take time on the linear plane." I listened intently, and assented by nodding my head. This was OK, I could do this.

"Be aware of all things animate and inanimate," Barnabas continued. "Be aware that nature has much to teach you, what your people have learned to overlook. Watch the seasons by paying attention to the littlest images in front of you. Look at nature's colors, and where the color is. Pay attention to the heavens, and the waters, the mirrors of heaven." I smiled at this, reflecting upon my love of being in water, and sailing small boats at our local boat club not far from our home.

"Pay attention to events celestial and physical—by this I mean, watch how nature and man connect. All things do not happen by chance." This was my first understanding of what I was to later grasp what he meant by how celestial events reflect what would occur on Earth. What the Chaldeans, the Babylonians, the Asians have known about astronomy/astrology, as they were one and the same in the past. He continued, "Do not worry so much about appearances. God, the Universal Presence, does not care about your image. It is what matters in the heart and the head that is important. That which is veridical is empirical." I could feel the skin over my heart warm, and the crown of my head felt as though a spinning vortex of energy spiraled, tingling inside and out.

"I will come and help you when you call me, but I will not always be at your 'beck and call.' He paused, adding, "There will be another Master who will teach you things for your own good. He will come when you least expect. Be appropriate and appreciative of what God has given you. I will always be near. God's grace on thee." With this first lecture, I threw myself into my book learning. I was to not hear again from Barnabas until 1988, and this coincided with the next Master—Master Yogananda—who appeared right out of thin air. For the next decade, I found myself working mainly in deep trance with Barnabas. Afterwards he decided to take a vacation for a decade, letting me grow on my own. Now that our darkroom group has earnestly begun sitting every Thursday, Barnabas has come to speak to our group, encouraging our efforts. He has spoken to me, waiting upon me to allow him to channel through once more to audiences with his comforting wisdom.

Saint Barnabas icon

Saint Barnabas' face impressed upon a silk precipitation,

through the mediumship of Reverend Hoyt Robinette.

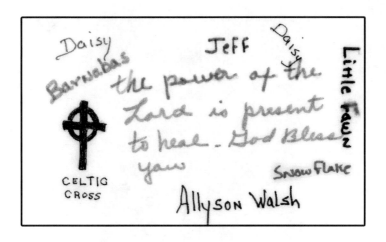

Card received where Barnabas indicated his last earth life in Ireland,
through the mediumship of Reverend Hoyt Robinette.

Jesus with the apostles. Barnabas in foreground with hand outstretched.
Mediumship of Hoyt Robinette.

Allyson—Master Yogananda

Years would speed by while I got married again in 1984 to a man named Patrick Walsh, whom I met through an acquaintance from ballroom dancing. David H. introduced us at a party. While looking at Patrick, I had one of those rare moments where the room felt like it was spinning, with walls falling away. It was as though time was going though a 'free-fall'—it seemed I met Patrick somewhere else in time. I didn't know it then, until several weeks after we started dating, that I then realized how I knew Patrick. I was getting dressed for a date with him one evening when suddenly the open closet door became the threshold to an open air plaza, across the Atlantic to what was then known as 'Thrace,' an ancient Grecian colony now known as Bulgaria. How did I know it was 'Thrace?' It was a 'knowing,' viewing myself now dressed unlike my modern-day counterparts. Dressed in a long, flowing dress with sandals, I watched in horror as men in white togas with sandals stormed my doorway, waving sticks. I recall that I was screaming, with a baby in my arms. As quickly as the image came, it left! I slammed the closet door shut, just as the Thracian men were coming at me. The room again became 1984, but it took a few minutes to get my nerves back! I had the feeling that those men were out to kill me and my husband, why I wasn't sure, and I didn't want to open up the past to find out!

I confidently let Patrick know within two dates that he was dating a woman with psychic abilities, and that if he was not comfortable with that, there was the door! I am certain that he was taken aback with my self-assuredness, but he believed that he could live with that. That didn't turn out to be the case in later years.

Our marriage proceeded well over the early years. Patrick was a tee-totaler, and had a bright career as a mechanical engineer with Westinghouse. He was part Irish, part Austrian/German. He was good-looking, looking very much like Jean-Claude Van Damme, the actor. One dark spot, though, tarnished our relationship, which later proved to drive us apart—his family was largely centripetal in that they depended solely on each other, and no other, for association. I was introduced to his mother on Mother's

Day several months after we started our relationship, and it was clear that 'outsiders' would never be privy to the family. Mom Walsh made it clear she disapproved of me for the simple reason that Patrick and I lived together for three years before marrying. What amazed me about her attitude was that we were both in our thirties! Mom Walsh had serious health issues with diabetes, which affected her eyesight. It was not long after that she dropped dead from an aneurysm. She didn't live long enough to see us married. Patrick, like Bernie, had a father that didn't live long enough to see his grown children. Shortly after his mother's passing, Patrick transferred pent-up anger and rage that festered under his collar for many years towards his mother to me. Patrick, like Bernie, wouldn't (or couldn't) talk about his problems, and thus spent fruitless years sulking and brooding over what he couldn't change. I have wondered if there was some karma in my attraction to men whose fathers died young, only to leave the women in charge, and their sons not able to grow up.

While we were engaged, Patrick was happy that I had a thriving free-lance graphic art production business, but he wanted a business of his own. He chose to sell Amway. It wasn't so much the Amway products that I disapproved of, it was the business practices that alarmed me (lying to people about what the business was about). Some of the Amway 'diamond' people were so shallow that they could have been cardboard paper cut-outs. It was during this time that I met Jim H., a man that Patrick wanted to recruit into the Amway business. It didn't work, but Patrick told Jim that his girlfriend was psychic, so Jim was intrigued enough to have us over for dinner to size me up. Jim, a dark haired, yellow-eyed man in his mid-twenties, asked me after dinner if I could tell him who would win the football game blaring on the television in his living room. More annoyed than anything, I silently asked Spirit to show me the winning numbers, and they came—16 to 6. But who was playing? I didn't know, so I asked Jim not to give me names of teams, but provide me the colors. What I remember now is that the Oakland Raiders—in black and silver colors—won the game 16 to 6. Jim couldn't believe it! He was fairly bouncing off the walls, while I was mildly impressed with my spirit guides. Now Jim wanted me to read for him. This I wasn't so wild to do, as I had never read for anyone before—I was able to get information for me, but never for others. All I had to do was ask.

I told Jim H. that I saw him moving out of the apartment that year, but not before he would have a 'falling-out' with his roommate. I didn't hear from Jim until six months later when he called, reporting that he had an argument with his roommate over an exorbitant telephone bill of his own making. Jim was presently calling me from the condominium he bought. Because of Jim, I started receiving people calling me for readings, and I scheduled them around my graphic arts business. This was the beginning of my psychic readings, and Jim, being the first person I read for, has been one of my greatest supporters throughout the years. It was also during this time that Barnabas, my Master Guide, came back into my life, and I found that during this period of time, I couldn't work so much in light-trance, but mostly in deep-trance—what people know as 'channeling.' Whether people believed he is real, I don't know, but I do know that he is real to me. More on Barnabas in another chapter.

Patrick wanted me to handle his business accounting books, but after I looked at how he handled his affairs on paper, I made it clear that I wouldn't be involved anymore, not when the IRS was breathing down his neck about Amway. This and the fact that as both my graphic arts and psychic reading businesses grew, he became more distant and angry. Patrick's need for a father figure, albeit gotten through the business scene, more or less superceded our relationship. Thereafter, I funneled more energy into my work.

Throughout the Eighties, I spent much time reading comparative religion books. Having been 'kicked out' of the Methodist church at the age of sixteen for being too inquisitive, I felt it was time to understand what many of the religions were about. By 1988, I was reading several spiritual books to help relieve stress that I felt was due to my workaholism and difficulties with Patrick. I picked up a paperback entitled, *Autobiography of a Yogi*, and tried to get through three chapters. I had such difficulty concentrating, so I put it away. Being a speed-reader since the ninth grade, no one was more surprised than I that I had no facility reading this book! I also made the decision by the end of that year to give up my graphic arts free-lance business to work full-time for one of my clients, one of the biggest medical publishers in the world. Strangely, Barnabas had warned me three years earlier that I would willingly 'walk away' from the graphic production business—I was told this during a deep-trance session in front of some trusted friends. Why was I doing this—going to work for a client? By May of 1989 I 'burned-out.' The medical publishing company worked me close to 60 hours a week. I tried to accommodate my other clients as well, which didn't leave me much time for a life, much less my relationship with my husband. Anyone who has experienced 'burn-out' will tell of feeling exhausted, and having no enthusiasm to continue. I could no more look at a magazine, much less a logo design, than to think about creating anything on paper. Forget about computers—I didn't have time in the previous years to learn graphic arts production on computers. I felt very much adrift, and my only anchor was to continue with the readings.

After I left the publishing company in June 1989, I picked the *Autobiography of a Yogi* book up again, and something astonishing happened. Not only could I now read the book, I found that I 'understood' Hindi and Sanskrit words without looking them up. What's more, I became so engrossed in reading Paramahansa Yogananda's *Autobiography* that I could hardly put it down. I would find myself reading and rereading chapters of his book—I was drinking in his wisdom. During this same time period, I found East Indian people would walk up and talk to me, even though we were complete strangers. I became entranced with Indian food. I felt that something important was happening, although I wasn't prepared for what was about to commence.

In August, I was laying on my bed upstairs in the early evening starting chapter seven of the *Autobiography*. I just finished rereading chapter six, and noticed car lights swiftly moving around the room. Noticing dusk on the western horizon, I knew that I would have to get up and turn lights on, but I hoped to get part of the next chapter read, so I focused on the book. As I was lying on my stomach, I finally glimpsed a light behind me getting brighter, not disappearing like the other lights. As my consciousness became more aware of the light, I slowly turned, swinging my legs over the side of the bed. Through the setting sun's dimming rays, I witnessed three men standing in the corner of the bedroom, but they were not life-size! In fact, they were not even opaque. Parts of them were transparent; their forms drifted hazily above the floor. The man in the middle was young—about twenty years old, with long black hair, and bright, intense eyes staring at me, his hands and head leaning on a straight staff. To his right stood a stalwart, tall man with a severe face, white hair and beard. The other man was smaller, looking more oriental than the others. All three were wearing ochre-colored robes. I recall that as I took my eyeglasses off, as I could see them clearly with 'stereoscopic vision,' meaning that my eyesight was better than 20/20. I could see minute details. What drew my attention more than anything else was what I call 'living fire' behind these stalwart figures. This fire moved, undulated, and shimmered, while the men never moved. We stared at each other for about ten minutes, for what seemed like centuries. I knew that I somehow recognized them, and I knew that they were reading me. A higher form of silent communication was transpiring! As the setting sun drew down over the horizon, the astonishing vision of the three men faded like a scroll rolling up. I pensively rose and went downstairs to wash leftover dishes from dinner. I didn't know how to feel about what I just saw, much less say anything to Patrick about it! It was several days before I cautiously picked the book up again (I wondered if they would appear again) to continue reading. Enthusiastic about reading this tome, I didn't know yet how Yogananda would influence my life.

Yogananda has appeared to me five times up to the publication of this book. Four times he etherealized, pulling his atoms subtly together to resurrect his physical form in transparent tone. He would visit when I least expected him. Only once, did I summon him by petitioning earnestly through meditation a need for an answer. When I did this, I saw him in the dark of the night at three in the morning. Etherealized from the waist up, he waved to me as though to 'come' to him, which I took as a good sign. I got the feeling, though, that I should not do this too often, as he seemed mentally very busy! Interestingly, *Mejda*, a book written by Yogananda's brother, Sananda Lal Ghosh, opened up for me an aside about his personality, which Yogananda did not cover in his *Autobiography*. It turns out that he was very interested in mediumship (although his teacher, Sri Yukteswar thought it to be a distraction from Yogananda's development, and I understand what he meant by this). Yogananda had a penchant for being very jovial; he liked to play practical jokes occasionally. In one of his five visits, he did exactly that!

The summer of 1994 had me visiting Camp Chesterfield of Chesterfield, Indiana, to unwind, take some spiritual classes, and have readings from mediums that worked at the camp. I saw six different mediums that week for readings, and all were good—my brother Jeff came through in more than two readings. One day that week was overcast; a bright white sky with over 55% humidity in the air. A perfect August afternoon for Indiana. I was in the cafeteria eating lunch, counting down the minutes before I headed over to see Pat Kennedy for a reading. Thinking I had better go to the women's bathroom before seeing her, I unloaded my lunch tray, and found myself moments later sitting on a commode in the women's bathroom. Much to my surprise, Yogananda's face appeared through the lavatory stall, and in my state of undress, my hands flew to my face in shock. I yelled out, "Oh, Yogananda!" I was horrified that he would see me this way! Yogananda laughed a shrill giggle, and simply said, "Oh, Brahmacharya!" I couldn't move. I couldn't look at him, as I was so embarrassed. Moments later, I tentatively looked around—Yogananda was no longer there. I hurriedly got dressed, and ran across the campground's pastoral green field to Pat Kennedy's house. She saw me coming, and was delighted that I was so enthusiastic! I raced in her door. Pat wrote down my name and birth date, to start what for her was a numerological beginning to her reading.

As she began her talk, though, it became clear that a great deal of noise on the tin roof of her house would impede our ability to continue. Pat asked if I would open the front door, look out, and see what was happening. We couldn't look out her windows to see, because at that time, her house had heavy draperies. I opened the front door, peered out, but I didn't see anything unusual. I turned to let Pat Kennedy take a look-see, and she huffed, "No, no, walk out in front of the house, turn around, and see what is going on!" I ventured out, and to my amazement, I saw a rain cloud, and only one, small enough to rain on the roof of Pat Kennedy's house! Reader, if you have read Paramananda Yogananda's *Autobiography of a Yogi*, you would understand that something like this happened to Sri Yukteswar by his teacher, Sri Lahiri Mahasaya. It was a sign of blessing! With joy, I bounced into the house, flopping into Pat's chair, laughing. Pat Kennedy stood at the door, then strode over to her desk and asked me (her eyes white on all sides) if I had an 'Eastern Indian master' working with me. She claimed she could smell sandalwood incense. I caught only a small whiff of it then, but in another occasion in Germany, with other people present, I sensed through the olfactory nerves the soothing sense of sandalwood.

As we sat down to begin the reading again, Pat claimed, "He calls you a name starting with the letter 'B.'" I was comforted by the fact that Yogananda was close by, that he was happy for me to have found my home (for the time being) within mediumship. I also knew that I would be learning more from Yogananda in the future. I was curious about what Yogananda called me when I was at the mediums camp—he used the word 'Bramacharya,' and I was not familiar with this Indian word. Two weeks later, I traveled to Virginia Beach, Virginia, and stopped into the Heritage Bookstore, one of the largest metaphysical bookstores on the East Coast. Wonder of wonders, while there I found there an English to Sanskrit—Sanskrit to English dictionary! Quickly I looked up this word, and found it indicates 'celibate student of God,' and 'teacher of creation.' How interesting! Was this to mean that I was a 'brahmacharya' from a past existence or this life?

Paramahansa Yogananda came to me in dreams for about a year thereafter to reintroduce me to the concept of Kriya Raja Yoga. I have not been able to remember any conversation from the dreams, only the postures and mudras (hand positions) that he showed me. I do remember he called this form of meditation the 'Key of Life,' which I was to later correlate to 'chi,' the oriental word for 'breath.' I started meditating and found that it helped focus my mental clarity, and as a side bonus, it helped my psychic gifts. I concentrated on the meditation for months, and clients asked me to teach them what I was doing. Again, I was somewhat reluctant, as I didn't have formal training in this, but if it helped others, why not? People started coming out of the woodwork to learn this breath-control. I was quietly amazed, and acknowledged that Yogananda himself must have been whispering to people in their minds to learn.

I taught meditation classes in several bookstores, in which two students of the 'Key of Life™' seminar asked me after a class was over, "If I understood what kind of yoga meditation that I was teaching?" A bold question! I answered that I stated in the beginning of the course how I received the teaching, and what I was told to call it. One of the students then blurted, "What you are teaching, especially those of the mudras, is about five thousand years old. You are teaching some of the oldest postures known as Kriya Raja Yoga. Look this up." With that, these two students, who obviously came and took the course to see what I knew about meditation, left, never to be seen again.

Undaunted, I spent time haunting bookstores looking for the subject of Kriya Raja yoga. Living in Baltimore in the late Eighties, without much about this subject in the New Age aisles of bookstores, I finally found a book by Swami Nikhilananda, entitled, *Vivekananda: The Yogas and Other Works*. Vivekananda had the same fiery 'alive' look in his eyes that I saw in Paramahansa Yogananda. The section on Raja Yoga seared me like a knife in my heart—I found what Yogananda wanted me to find. This form of yoga meditation fit me like a groove, and has always centered me in my soul. I hope to write a book about Kriya Raja yoga in a Western-styled format someday. Meditation is still the anchor of my life.

In 1989 I taught 60 people altogether in one day many of the secrets to the Key of Life™ yoga meditation. The class was taught north of Baltimore in a mansion, in one of the wings built with real Tiffany glass in windows, fireplace, as well as some original Tiffany tables. The floor of the room we occupied was polished gray marble; the room gave one the impression of a modernized medieval church setting. During one of our mantra sessions, next to where I stood teaching, a pillar candle flared up with the fire reaching to the heavens four inches high! There was a rumbling noise that sounded like the pouring of water, but the candle didn't melt. I was not the only one in the room to see and hear the candle; however, not all were privy to the spirit demonstration! For four days afterwards, attendees called to tell me how euphoric they felt. My belief is that Yogananda blessed us with his noncorporeal presence.

Paramahansa Yogananda again appeared to me in 1999 at a Unity Church in Severna Park, where a friend invited me to attend Sunday church services. My friend Deborah steered me into a row of seats where I sat on the outer right-hand side of the chapel, Deborah was to my left. I enjoyed listening to the lay leader throughout the service, but I was surprised to find a silent meditation was called. We all sat concentrating our thoughts for approximately fifteen minutes.

It was during this meditation that I focused my eyes on the horizon, lifting them gently upwards behind closed eyelids. I stayed this way for about five minutes, working on clearing my mind. Like a mist taking form, a face took shape as though it was a foot away from mine—it was Paramahansa Yogananda as he looked in his last year on earth. I was startled to see him looking at me so closely, yet I was so pleased. I opened my eyes to see his dazzling form standing in the outer aisle, ten feet in front of me! This has been the only time to date that I have seen Sri Yogananda materialized as solid as we all were in that chapel. His ocher swami clothing, the western-styled pants and wingtip shoes—all that he wore formed down to the last thread. He stood smiling at me for about ten minutes. A flood of feeling, an outpouring from Yoganandaji (a term of respect, utilizing his name) surrounded me, and my heart expanded to engulf the room. We shared no words, but we shared infinite space! I wanted to get up to hug him, but paralyzed, I could not move. His bemused look remained all those momentous minutes. Eventually I was able to move my left arm to poke Deborah, trying to get her to open her eyes, but alas, in vain, she wouldn't stir. I gave up, knowing then that Yoganandaji did this for my benefit. We shared a silent mental dialogue for a few more minutes, until his effulgence faded. First his feet and legs, then his torso melted away, until all that remained before me was the empty aisle whereupon he stood. I sat still in a half-stupor for a minute more, before the Unity ministering leader moved to stir the audience. What few minutes remained of the church service left me with a cold feeling in the pit of my stomach, due to the strangeness of my experience.

After the church service was over, I asked my friend Deborah why she wouldn't look at me when I poked her arm earlier. She said this slowly, as if in a reverie, "I don't know—I knew something was going on in the aisle next to you, but I couldn't get my eyes to open." Yogananda's influence allowed her to know that 'something' was happening, but my great guru mentor had the last laugh. It was also the last time Paramahansa Yogananda appeared to me, but I sit in meditation today, waiting to see his Grace once more.

One of the more incredible, colorful card precipitations ever created through the mediumship of Reverend Hoyt Robinette, there are several meanings of this card. The card has a 'tarot card' look to it; perhaps Spirit is aware that Allyson Walsh wrote a book entitled, *The Sacred Tarot Unveiled*. A chambered nautilus shell spills the microcosm of the physical world into the foreground. A logo of a chambered nautilus is still used as artwork by Allyson. Her love of oriental philosophy is inspired by the Indian god Krishna and his consort Radha shown in devotion at the bottom of the card precipitation. The bear's meaning was for a time hidden, until Allyson realized that it was representative of her research of St. Brigit and King Arthur ('Arthur' was a Celtic title meaning "Great Bear") for a historical fiction book when she received this card.

Adele's Awakening

This particular chapter picks up when I, Adele, have been married for about sixteen years, with a growing family with a daughter aged nine, and a son of five years. We have a single-family home, both of us working out of the home to provide our family with the necessities of life.

Since childhood, my sister Allyson and I knew to keep our 'gift' a secret to ourselves once we began schooling; however, Allyson's ability to predict certain things in high school did surface. My ability was there, but being distracted by dating rituals of high school and college life, I needed space. Not that I did not want my 'gift,' but I knew that people would find me strange and not want to associate with me. I felt my spirit guides were waiting for the perfect moment to wake me up.

In my thirties, I willed my 'gift' away because of many demands on my time being a middle-school teacher, a wife and mother to two children. At home, once dinner was over, the burden of grading homework took over any playtime I could have had with my children. The nightly rituals were baths, lunches to make, pajamas to get into for bed. My husband did a great job of assuming responsibilities of the children when I had to prepare for school the next day.

Several incidents prepared me for my 'awakening.' I began to feel, see, and hear things around me. I would be working at the kitchen counter, and feel something touching my legs or ankles; sometimes water appeared on my legs or feet. A hand would touch me on my shoulder when there was no one in the kitchen with me. I would hear someone talk to me in my mind, and I would automatically know that it wasn't my own thoughts. I'd call my sister Allyson and relate to her what was happening to me. She encouraged me to meditate to help bring my gift along. I innately felt I would not have to—my spirits would bring it along in their fashion. Not that I had much time to meditate anyway.

Other things happened to get my attention in the house. I heard a man's voice call my name out loud and clear, yet there was no one but me in the bedroom, as my husband had already left for work. I explained it away, thinking it was all 'in my head.' I had recently bought some hallway rugs for the upstairs hallway, adjoining three bedrooms. I placed them upstairs when my sister Allyson came over for a visit. My two children were playing in the house, when I took my sister upstairs. To my surprise, the hallway rugs were at the bottom of the stair landing! I remember remarking to my sister that this was strange, but I asked my children if they had moved the rugs to the stairway landing. Looking at the reaction of their faces, I knew they had no idea what I was talking about, as they had been playing in the basement. Spirit was beginning to move other things as well.

Kitchen items were known to move around especially when my sister Allyson would come over for a visit. My sister would occasionally glance into the kitchen while we were conversing in the living or dining rooms, and once she casually mentioned that spoons lifted off the counter, floating in thin air!

Another remembrance involved my twin sister staying overnight at my home. My daughter, twin sister, and I were lounging in the living room talking past midnight, when all of us felt a deep cold creep up our ankles past our knees. My daughter, not accustomed to physical phenomena as yet, exclaimed, "Do you feel that? It's cold in here all of a sudden!" Without hesitation, muffled male voices, along with the sound of snuffling horses crossed the room. All of us sensed several Indian men and a horse litter dragging across a 'trail' parallel to the room. The movement and sound was unquestionable; all of our heartbeats were palpable.

Allyson had the initiative to speak out loud, "Whoever you are, you are welcome to pass by!" The voices and litter stopped; it was obvious 'they' heard us. Pregnant moments passed before they moved onward. My daughter and I sat immobile in our seats—Allyson, on the other hand, looked elated and relaxed. "How about that," she chortled. "We were visited by American Indians!" Looking back, this was their first visit, but not their last.

I remember Allyson telling me that it would be a matter of time before we would be working together in front of people. I wasn't so sure, initially—it was all I could do to deal with my present situation in life. Yet, one particular time in my early thirties, while preparing to get ready for work in early hours, I felt someone *push* me between my shoulder blades towards the bathroom sink and mirror! This incidence reoccurred five to seven more times that month (after our talk of working jointly) in the morning, with my finally exclaiming out loud, "All right! I will join Allyson to work together!" After exclaiming this, the pushing stopped.

One night while we were asleep, a mantle clock that sat on a corner cupboard came crashing noisily down to the floor around two in the morning. Jolted out of bed by the deafening sound, my husband and I cautiously crept downstairs to see what happened. The clock indeed was listing on its side, with the chimes still reverberating from the fall. We both looked at each other in amazement because there was no way that the clock could have fallen by itself. It would have had to slide off the cupboard five inches from the edge to drop. I knew that spirits were doing this to get our attention.

The last straw was a goose decoy that I had crafted and displayed on the shelves behind our queen-size bed. One night I awoke to something hitting my face, landing around my shoulders. I yelled out, waking my husband, Douglas. He hurriedly turned on the bedside lamp; Doug sleepily wanted to know what was in bed with us. As I placed the decoy in another part of the bedroom, I silently knew spirits were being mischievous, doing everything they could to get my notice.

Chief Red Cloud, shown here young and old, adding his name to Adele's card precipitation, through the mediumship of Reverend Hoyt Robinette.

At Allyson's urging, I met a medium that Allyson brought in from Camp Chesterfield, Indiana. Hoyt Robinette came to Allyson's house in 1995, to present a different form of mediumship. Hoyt is a physical phenomena medium, specializing in 'card precipitation,' which allows spirit helpers and artists write names and messages on cards, often with drawings, paintings, and scotographs. (A scotograph is a spirit 'photograph' that is lifted from an actual photograph, however, there are often small changes seen in the scotograph). There is no human involvement with the writing on the cards, spirit does this exclusively. Hoyt acts as the catalyst for the phenomena. With curiosity and some skepticism I watched Hoyt the first time he explained to the group of people present how this is done. As he had someone in the session open a brand-new pack of 3" x 5" blank index cards, he explained that all of the writing utensils had their caps or tops on, as spirit pulls the essence of the color from the barrels of the pens and pencils (which were not sharpened) to 'write' or 'draw' on the cards. After he displayed the tightly woven snake basket with its lid to everyone present, he took a few cards and utensils, and layered them all back into the basket until it was full. He put the lid firmly on the basket, and set it to the side, fully visible to all of us that were there. There was low-level light in the room, as Allyson had two or three lamps on so that we could all see what was happening. In these sessions, we would get a short psychic message from Hoyt. Sometimes Hoyt would wear a blindfold with taped eyes, delivering messages from holding a folded 'billet,' which is a piece of paper with one's name on it, including names of loved ones that have passed, and a question enclosed. Hoyt would hold and feel the billet, to get the 'vibration' of the spirit who was talking to him, giving him answers. It was wonderful! Some of the card precipitations are included here for you to peruse.

These sessions with Hoyt Robinette taught me who some of my guides are. Allyson and I share Master Barnabas, although he works more often with my sister. I learned of two prominent American Indians, Chief Red Jacket and Chief Red Cloud, who work with me. They have been with me for some time helping me to understand my life, teaching me patience! Chief Red Jacket likes to travel in the car with me, often telling me which roads to travel to avoid accidents—he helps me find parking spaces in crowded parking lots! Red Jacket is good-natured and free-wheeling, wanting to go places and do things. Red Cloud is calm, wise and patient; he tells me things about future events. On card precipitations received through the years, my spirit guides and relatives signed their names on the backside of the card drawings. A picture of Red Cloud appeared on a spirit card that was 'lifted' out of a small American Indian photo book that Allyson gave me years ago; I kept it stashed in my teaching desk. When I received the spirit card, Red

Cloud spoke to me inwardly, "Adele, you have the same picture in a book you own." I found the book at school, only to realize that the picture was scotographed identically to the spirit card given to me earlier!

Chief Red Cloud and Chief Red Jacket were North American Indian chieftains who lived in the nineteenth century. Red Jacket was a Canadian Indian who rose to prominence with the American government. He helped with the plight of Canadian and American Indians of the Northeast territory. Red Cloud was a powerful leader of the Sioux nation, known for his resistance to white occupation of the Dakota Territory, and later for his attempts to secure peaceful relations between his people and the United States government.

Having these two Indians for my guides has been 'powerful medicine' for me. Every person has at least seven guides in their life that give guidance (whether the person is aware of them or not). Having the two Indian chiefs guide me has been a blessing. Another spirit guide I was to meet is a 'joy guide' named 'Singing Bird.' Joy guides belong to the angelic kingdom; they are attached to physical nature, and they are part of the four elements—earth, air, fire, and water. Certain cultures refer to these guides as fairies, elves; others call them 'devas,' which means, 'shining ones.' Joy guides are here to bring us joy and happiness in various ways. Singing Bird brings me feathers, and at times birds come up to me, not afraid to be near me. This is because Singing Bird envelopes her energy around birds. Blue Jays, cardinals, robins, and chickadees are plentiful around my house; they fill the air with their song!

Several of our 'dead' relatives have their names imprinted on the spirit cards, in order to let Allyson and I know that they are watching over our family. All of us have our spirit guides and loved ones watching and helping us. People may not understand this fact, but they selflessly guide us nonetheless.

One evening, Allyson invited me to join several of her students to hear Janet Cyford speak, a British medium who authored the book entitled, *A Ring of Chairs*. Janet went around the group and spoke individually to each person about their guides. When she came to me, she stated, "You have an Indian that has the color 'red' in his name and as part of his clothing. Do you know who he is?" I nodded, and replied, "Yes! It's Chief Red Jacket!" I was thrilled that he had come. Janet added, "You know he is your protector, don't you? He is here to help you along your path. He will prove to you that all of this is real."

As the evening wound down, I told my sister I needed to get home quickly, as I had to get up early for work. While driving, I spoke out loud to my protector guide Chief Red Jacket to get me home as the hour was late. I was heading north on Route 2 through the Severna Park area, knowing that it would take me about twenty minutes to get home. Traffic on the divided highway was brisk, even at nine o'clock at night. I decided to turn left on Route 2 at a particular intersection that has a long traffic light sequence. Knowing that I might have to sit for several minutes waiting for the light to turn green for me, I shouted to my Indian in my mind, "Chief Red Jacket! If you are truly there, make the light change faster so I can get home—I need to be in bed!" Suddenly, the left turn signal turned green, and as I sped across the highway, I looked back. To my surprise, traffic was still moving down the south side of Route 2, which meant that my guide had interfered with the mechanization of the traffic signal in order to get me home! As soon as I got in my door, I called Allyson, exhilarated, and related what had happened. I exclaimed, "I will never disbelieve again! I know now indeed that there *is* more than the physical world around us!"

Some time later I timidly joined my sister one night at one of the bookstores, where Allyson had a platform message circle to conduct. With some nervousness, I went with Allyson to use my 'psychic sense' in front of strangers. As we sat down with our chairs moved into a large circle, my sister began to introduce herself. Allyson then told the group that I was joining her to help in giving psychic messages.

Surprisingly, I found my nervousness left me, as I was hearing thoughts and phrases being put into my mind as my sister talked to the audience. I delivered one particular person the message I was given, with the idea that the recipient would understand what the message meant to him. A sense of tranquility, or peacefulness overcame me. Giving messages produces an overshadowing sense of heat or cold as we work. Allyson attributes this to the spirits working with us, that spirits lower their electromagnetic energy to work 'between the worlds' for spirit communication.

When we left the bookstore that night, I had a strong sense of exhilaration, knowing that we helped people in different ways. Allyson knew that my working with her would strengthen our combined psychic sense in future groups. Not in my wildest dreams did I ever realize that this would definitely come true as we began to work with small and large audiences.

Allyson—Spirit "Follows" Through

These anecdotal incidents appear on the surface strange and coincidental, but in hindsight, a lesson is learned from them. I recount them as being true and factual, and unless you have had similar circumstances, there will be those individuals who will not believe.

The first event occurred when Barnabas, my Master Guide and spirit companion, helped me with a situation that showed me how *not* in-control-of-everything I am. This was 1988, and a woman I vaguely knew as Glenda U., called to make an appointment for a reading. I gave her a date and time. The day of her reading, Glenda called 45 minutes before her appointment to tell me that she would not be able to come. When I asked why, she stated, "Oh, one of my grandkids is not feeling well. I have been babysitting them this morning, and their mother is not back yet, so I had better not come!" Yes, I was a little peeved for the late call, but there was an underlying itch that got to me, and I didn't know why. I hung up the phone. Now free to pursue other matters, I had an overwhelming urge, a push, to go Golden Ring Mall, minutes away.

I jumped into my car and sped up the road. Traffic was light, and I had no pressing matters for a few hours. It had been ages since I went window-shopping. In no time I was walking around in the mall, checking out the latest fashions, getting something to nibble on, casually strolling around.

Sometimes when I think hard about something, I find that I have a tendency to look at the ground, just in front of my moving feet. This was just such a moment in the Mall. Without paying too much attention to where I was heading, I almost crashed into two women with two strollers. One of them was Glenda U, with daughter and grandchildren in tow. The look on Glenda's face was priceless! Her face was shocked, even bloodless. Her sudden knowledge of me in front of her drained her, looking helpless. She stumbled to introduce her daughter to me, stammering pathetically, "What are you doing here? How did you know that I would be here?" as if thinking that I must have followed her, but not quite sure.

I looked levelly at her, and for a moment, I felt as though I was looking right through her. Without a moment's hesitation, I realized that Barnabas, in spirit, led me straight to her, to catch her in her outright lie to me! In understanding her desperate knowledge of her deception, and unable to escape the situation, the realization of this rendezvous sent shockwaves and chills through my body. My hair on the nape of my neck stood on end. The feeling was of a quantity of adrenalin pumping in me. Was this knowledge powerful? Yes. What would I do about it? I wasn't sure.

Glenda, unable to look me in the eyes, looked around from side to side, at the ground, anywhere but at me. She knew she was caught in the lie, and there was no way out. The moment presented clearly ramifications of power, and I saw how those in powerful positions would use this to their advantage—they would exact revenge verbally and/or physically. I could see in this moment of clarity how much of humanity reacts this way. Yet, what I chose was 'grace,' the ability to let her have mercy, not put her down in front of her daughter and others in the mall. I had no need to make a scene, the 'scene' was already over. The lesson learned by Glenda—do not deceive to cover what you really want to do! This left her in a vulnerable position as she was found out, and I trust that her learning was deep. I acted very casual in my reaction, but cool. I did not let on about what happened, nor raise my voice. I coolly asked Glenda how she was, and moved on through the mall, waving goodbye. I never saw her again.

Curiously, Glenda advertised herself as an instructor of metaphysics. She taught many courses out of her house in Essex, Maryland. I attended a class taught by a practitioner of numerology at her house. My initial meeting of Glenda was at that class, and I believed (at that moment) she was a decent person. I still think she is, but I heard from other people who attended functions with her that she, like many others in the New Age movement, set themselves up as 'gurus.' She wasn't the first, nor will be the last. It escapes me why people do what they do. Many individuals who want power and glory from having small portions of spiritual knowledge miss the mark. There is no power or glory to be achieved. Truly enlightened spiritual teachers do not put the spotlight upon themselves; they attribute the Universal Force (God/Goddess) as the sole Power and Glory. True power is gained in putting others first, achievement is gained on another level through service to others. Quoting the Master Jesus, "The first shall be last, and the last shall be first," as he spoke to his disciples. The lesson given to me by my Master guide Barnabas, was indeed profound—a lesson learned at the knees of a teacher in spirit.

The second account is from the time I initially worked in light trance. In a previous chapter, I disclose how Barnabas saved my life from a potential car accident, and how he began to teach me between the ages of sixteen and twenty. Barnabas came back into my life one day when I was about 35 years of age, married to my second husband Patrick, and living in the city of Baltimore. My graphic art production work was steady; financially I was content. I was starting to give psychic readings due to my reading my first client, Jim H., and word-of-mouth advertising about my psychic counseling spread quickly. I recall two early clients that I read during these early years—one was an older female, Sadie, about 85 years of age, with a chip on her shoulder. The other was a stout woman named Judith, in her thirties. I recall the first woman because of her insistence upon hearing from a particular person in spirit, and I was not experienced enough at this point to realize that I was in charge!

As I was new to the work, I thought I had to have her sit about ten feet away from myself. Once positioned, I explained to her that I would bring through for her one or two from spirit. I told her that I could not guarantee to bring in an 'expected' spirit; we would have to see who showed up. Even so, Sadie was not happy; she demanded that she hear from someone she expected. As she spoke, over top of her voice I heard a male voice calling out his name 'Walter.' He was insistent, so much so that he repeated his name over and over. His persistence was so strong, that he vehemently 'poured' what felt like hot water over the crown of my head, down the right ear! The pain was real—I bolted out of the chair, yelling out loud, "Walter, why did you do this? I was going to say your name! That was not necessary!" Sadie, with a derisive exclamation, said, "What! Walter, my good-for-nothing brother-in-law? I don't want to hear from him, I want to hear from my mother!" Sadie stood up as well, and for a moment, I realized I was losing control of the situation. I calmed her down, letting her know that Walter was here because he wanted to be heard. I don't recall much more of that reading, but she stated afterwards that her mother never came through any of the psychics she visited. I imagine I wasn't the last. Once she left, though, I inwardly thanked Walter for coming for her (I forgave him for the hot water treatment!). I could well imagine why he was there for her—their temperaments were as much alike as peas in a pod! Sadie and Walter were disagreeable people, in life and in spirit. I ascertained that Sadie's mother had 'moved on' without the need to stay behind to help influence her obstinate daughter. I was to later find that this happens in many instances.

Judith would become of my more dramatic cases, as it was the first time my Master guide took control of my body to speak through my vocal cords. This was an instance of Barnabas, Dr. Albertson, and his team introducing me to deep-trance channeling. The Divine Hand was instrumental in rescuing an overweight, depressed woman whose life was endangered by her impending decisions. Spirit needed to speak to her directly; and I would learn later that using me as the 'go-between' was necessary to reach her. It was another moment that taught me *I am not in control of this work*.

Judith came one languid summer day in 1985 to my house in Baltimore city from the Washington, D.C. area—my first client from there. She lumbered in the door, sat down in my rocking chair, while I settled myself on the couch, moving into a light meditative trance. I glanced at Judith, asked her to say her name and her birth date, when I started to feel my eyes roll back into my head. I fought the urge to do this, and yet found myself saying to Judith, "I will meditate a few minutes, so wait until you hear me speak." She nodded; she had never seen me before, what did she know about how I worked? In truth, I usually worked in 'light trance,' which is to say that I am conscious, albeit not far from drowsing, as if in a very light sleep state. Secondly, I never worked in a deep-trance state before, so how did I know that this was what was about to happen? Upon a moment of reflection, I realized something unusual was about to happen, and I was not happy to find out!

The reason I say that I knew something unusual was happening, was because there were balls of light appearing in the house for several hours prior to our session. As I was still involved with graphic art production at this time, working over my drafting board, I would have light come up behind me such that it would cast shadows on the wall in front of me. When I would see this occurring, I would turn slightly to see from whence the light was projected, but as soon as I commenced the turn, the light would vanish. My husband Patrick, of course, never saw these balls of light. I learned over time, the light presaged an imminent paranormal incidence.

I told Judith that I would close my eyes to begin the session, so I politely asked her to be quiet for a few moments until I stirred. Judith agreed, so I closed my eyes. *Oh no, I am falling asleep!* My consciousness immediately was pushed out of the back of my head and neck. I felt like rushing wind leaving my body, whooshing through a narrow tunnel, to end up in an enormous amber light-field. Through my 'soul eyes' the illumination appeared to stretch to infinity! Amber, gorgeous amber light, everywhere! My consciousness seemed to be everywhere as well, as I could hear what was happening in a room far away, a room that had another voice speaking through my vocal cords to a discouraged, distraught woman named Judith. The voice, distinctly male with an Irish accent, spoke.

"Greetings lass, my name is Barnabas. I speak to you today through my Lady, as I have with me several physicians present to help with your reading and diagnosis. We cannot allow you to go forward with what you are on course to do, which is to end your life by the end of this week."

A great pause ensued; Judith did not react. I, on the other hand, when I heard this voice speaking through my vocal cords, yelled out, "WHAT? What is going on here? Get me back to my body!" I demanded this several times, all the while this other voice continued to talk to Judith in a reassuring way. "We cannot allow you to end your life—it is not time for you to cross over. Dr. Albertson, the chemist here, is giving me information to help with your condition. You have a problem with your thyroid, do you not?" Judith was shocked. Apparently, Barnabas, a spirit that I had forgotten about since I entered college, was presently involved, and jumping right into the fire with Judith! Out in my amber light-field, I was aware of all of this, and helpless to do anything but listen. Spirit wasn't ready to let me have control just yet!

Judith jumped out of the rocking chair, and yelled, "That's right, but how did you know that? I just found out that my thyroid is not normal yesterday! My life has just been hell for six years, and now this!" Well, I could have tripped over myself, if I was in my body. Barnabas continued, "How do we know? It is seen in your light, the light of your physical, emotional, mental and spirit bodies." I realized that what spirit was seeing was the 'aura' of Judith, and apparently, Barnabas and Dr. Albertson collaborated, scanning in her energy field a dark area, indicating a health issue. Now I was still, engrossed in what this spirit, Barnabas, had to say. Judith, energized, peppered Barnabas with questions, "What do you mean you can see the thyroid problem in my light? Is that like an X-ray to you? Is there a way for me to ever get better?" Barnabas cleared 'his' throat, stating, "You need to start seeing another kind of physician, you know this? The one you have been seeing for years has done you no good. Yes, you can get better with treatment and medication for the thyroid, but change is needed in your choice of physicians." He paused, as if listening, then added, "I understand that we will be helping from this side to see that this change occurs shortly. You will get your help from a biochemical doctor. We will be back to help you soon. God's grace on thee, lass. We must leave." With that, Judith watched as I crash-landed back into my body, just like a small airplane landing badly. Boy, did I have an instant headache! Judith was beside herself, asking me as I started to stir, waving her hands around, "How did you do that?" It was all I could do to answer her questions, and act as though what just transpired was normal. She was jubilant, even eager to write out a check, leaving shortly thereafter with me trying to figure out just what did happen. My head throbbed, and I went looking for pain reliever. I wondered to myself what had truly happened, and what if spirit was talking a lot of nonsense? While I was *wherever* I was when I was out of my body, I was yelling to myself, "I do *not* want to be an Edgar Cayce! I do not want that responsibility!" Edgar Cayce is considered the twentieth century's greatest 'sleeping prophet,' having had recorded over 14,000 medical and life readings, with many, many client testimonials to his veracity. I knew nothing of medicine, so why was this happening to *me*? But the deed was done, and that was that. I laid myself down gingerly on the same couch that this all transpired upon, wondering if some residual magical energy lingered!

Seven days passed. My husband was in the living room, his face covered with a section of the newspaper. Nothing unusual about this. It was about 10:30PM. I sat down on the couch, and noticed that the newspaper was not our usual Baltimore *Sun* paper. Patrick had picked up *The Washington Post*, unusual for him to do so. I remarked about this, and he said, "Oh, the *Sun* paper didn't come this morning, so I got this at work." I didn't know what section to look at, so I picked up the Business section, and briefly scanned the front and second page, until I got to the third page inside. A filler article having to do with 'depressed moms having low thyroid conditions' stood out to me, and as I read the contents of the article, suddenly a voice in my head shouted, "Call Judith! *Call Judith now!*" I knew that voice now, dropping the newspaper. I babbled to Patrick emphatically that I had to call someone. I went upstairs to my office, and looked for the check that Judith gave me (which I never cashed—I was afraid to) to see if I could find her phone number. No such luck. Without hesitation, I called Washington, D.C. information, and asked the operator if she was listed. I thought, "Women don't have their full names listed, especially in the cities." It turned out that I was wrong—the operator gave me the number immediately, which she dialed. Her phone rang three times, and there was Judith sleepily saying *hello*—I knew she was in bed. I exclaimed, "Judith, it is Allyson. I hope I didn't wake you, but I have something I need to tell you." I could feel a force well up from inside . . . I knew then that the 'voice' that was Barnabas was speaking in my head, and I heard myself tell her, "It has been a week since I saw you, but I know that the article in today's *Washington Post* is meant for you. Did you see it? If not, pull it out of the Business section, page 3, tomorrow, and show it to your doctor. It's important!" I stopped, hesitating for a moment to see if Judith would respond. She did. "Allyson, it's strange that you called me. My psychiatrist that I have been seeing for six years decided today that since I have now tested for low thyroid hormones, I will be seeing a biochemical specialist. I have the *Post*—I'll look at it tomorrow. Thanks for everything, goodbye." She hung up, going back to sleep, while I sat there listening to the dial tone for few moments. I realized then I was not in control of this work at all. A Divine Hand was intervening, and following through.

Another case where spirit followed through was an interesting woman named Dee Sears, who called in December 1999, asking for an appointment. I asked if she was referred by an existing client, she stated that she was. With the January appointment penned into my appointment calendar, I thought nothing more of this until our session. This was to prove to be another one of the more memorable sessions I have had, and because of it, I believe I reached a degree of graduation in my work.

Dee Sears with her son John walked in my door that cold January afternoon, stomping their feet, and huddling in their coats for a moment before taking them off. After our initial hellos, hanging coats in the closet, I offered refreshments out of courtesy, which were turned down. Dee blithely called out, "I am not sure why we are here today—my husband and I just came from seeing George Anderson in December. We waited up to a year on his waiting list before we could see him." I felt as though I got punched in my solar plexus—*Oh my God, they went to see George Anderson*! I felt light-headed, and walked into my kitchen for a moment to breathe. I quickly mumbled a prayer to God and the spirits to help me, as I knew that this was truly a test of my ability! I asked them to sit at my reading table, her son John to my left, with Dee right in front of me. What transpired next was most unusual, but a lesson for me!

Where Dee and John acted normal enough before our session, now both of them sat like stones throughout the reading. I tried to make it clear to them that I needed to hear their voices to hear spirit, but this fell on deaf ears. The best I could do during the session was to watch both of them just shake their heads up and down for 'yes,' or sideways for 'no.' As soon as I pitched to them how I work, I saw ectoplasm take shape next to Dee in the form of a young girl about eighteen. "All right, Dee and John, there is ectoplasm indicating a young girl or woman between the two of you. You lost a daughter, didn't you, Dee?" Her eyes watered, her mouth tightened, but Dee only shook her head *yes*, she wouldn't speak. I spoke up to them both, reminding them that I needed their voices to hear spirit, but they would not comply. As soon as I recognized the girl, I saw her leave her folks and move to my right side to speak. "She tells me that she died when she was about eighteen or nineteen years of age." I hoped that they would corroborate this. They did, again, with a headshake. "Would I be correct to say that she died from a problem with her blood—was it leukemia?" Again, the headshake, and now Dee asked me only one of the two questions she would ask in the entire session, "Do you get her name?" I looked at Dee; she had a strange, taunting look on her face. I thought, *oh Lord, what did I do to deserve this?* I felt that Dee was not as 'open' to the reading as I had hoped, and with her tightening up, I was concerned that I was becoming upset. When I get upset, I cannot work as well, so I had to work hard at ignoring her behavior and attitude, and pay attention to spirit.

I heard the girl in spirit fairly shout, "My name is Joanna Jill!" I repeated what I heard, and Dee gave me a hard look with a sideways 'no.' Frowning, I knew what I heard, and I was still hearing the girl repeat it several times, and I repeated it back to Dee. Again, she shook her head no, but wouldn't say anything. "Look," I said, "I am positive this is her name, or very close to that. She wants you to know that she wants me to see that there is a February birthday in this family, am I right?" John's eyes lit up, and he verbalized, "Yes, it is my Dad's birthday in February. What does she say about it?" I listened again. Finally, after a series of pictures and words in my mind, I was forthcoming with, "Your daughter wants me to say to you that she is going to do something for her Dad and his birthday. This may seem enigmatic, but I feel that she wants to keep this a surprise from all of you. It will be her 'gift' for her father." Both Dee and her son John looked at me with raised eyebrows, but said nothing. After a few more comments from her daughter, I wrapped up the session. I really felt that this session was onerous, and believed that I would never see these people again.

Imagine my surprise when I stood up, left the room, and Dee spoke, "Well, you got my daughter's name better than George Anderson." I stopped what I was doing, and came back into my reading room with a stunned look. "I thought you intimated that I got it wrong, Dee." I was perplexed at the sudden turnaround. Dee was now putting her coat on. Breathily, she said, "Well, you were close. Her name is Jenna Jill. She was 20 when she passed from a rare form of leukemia. George Anderson thought her name was Jennifer. You got it, I suppose." I informed Dee that spirit has to reference what names I know—"Jenna" was not a name I had heard before, so 'Joanna' was the closest name I would recognize. Dee shook her head positively that she understood, but didn't know why Jenna Jill was enigmatic about her message to the family. I said, "I don't know, Dee, but I suppose you will find out when Paul has his birthday." I paused for a moment, and boldly asked, "By the way—how much does George Anderson charge for his readings—I had no idea that you would have to wait so long to see him!" Dee was writing a check with a flourish, but she refused to tell me; she said she would have to think about whether she would tell me or not! Frankly, I was not amused, rather aggravated, and glad they both left!

Early March saw my birthday come and go. I answered the telephone one afternoon to hear the voice of Dee telling me, "Allyson, could you forgive me? If ever there was a way I could grovel over the telephone, this is it! I am so sorry that I treated you the way that I did when John and I came for our reading. I was so impolite! Jenna Jill gave us all a surprise when Paul's birthday came, just as you said she would. I would be glad to tell you what she did."

"Jenna Jill managed to influence not only John, but our other daughter and myself! What she did was put the idea of 'serenity' into all of our heads when we went looking for birthday cards or presents for my husband Paul. John found a father's birthday card with the headline of 'Serenity.' His sister gave her father a framed 'Serenity Prayer,' you know, the one used by Alcoholics Anonymous. I also gave Paul a birthday card that had the word 'serenity' it, but not one of us realized this until we presented them to my husband! When the realization came, John and I burst into tears, and we both knew then that Jenna Jill did *this* on purpose! I needed to tell you—it was the best present Jenna Jill gave all of us, and Paul is now healing from his grief. You see, Allyson, Paul was very close to Jenna, and lived in constant pain until the night of his birthday. What you gave us was a miracle, and I am so sorry for the way I treated you."

All I could do was listen in stunned silence.

"You asked me a question at the session that I refused to answer, and again, I am sorry, so I will tell you now. George Anderson charged my husband Paul and me one thousand dollars for a half-hour session. His assistant told us before we met with George—sit down, do not speak, and when the time is up, it is finished. I just didn't think that you would be as good, considering you charged one hundred dollars, but I made the appointment on a whim, and what a whim!"

After our goodbyes, I hung up the telephone, and chortled to the heavens, "OK, up there! Thanks to all of my guides and to you, Jenna Jill, for delivering an Oscar performance. I am proud of all of you!" I started back to my previous endeavor before the phone call, when I felt a light 'hand' on my shoulder. I heard in my mind, "Well done." Nothing more. A feeling of exhilaration warmed my heart—and the following day I raised my reading rate. I knew I 'graduated.' Spirit is the teacher, we learn what we will, and spirit follows through!

Adele—The Turning Point of Our Work Together

As we worked with small platform audiences in bookstores around Annapolis and Baltimore, I remarked to my sister that Spirit suggested that we needed to work in front of larger groups of people. In March of 2000, Allyson purchased tickets for our birthday to see Sylvia Brown, a nationally known psychic, who was visiting Washington, D.C. for a tour. Naturally we were excited about seeing her work in front of a large audience.

If anyone knows the configuration of Washington, D.C. streets, it can be rather daunting to find your destination if you are not familiar with the area. Needless to say, we traveled around the two main circles in town before we realized that the hotel address where the Sylvia Brown event was listed was incorrect. When we finally found the hotel and went to the door of the event, I gasped, because there must have been over eight hundred people in the large room. I remember telling my sister, "There are no seats left!" Allyson said to keep moving down the aisle, and we stopped in front of Sylvia Brown. Allyson then told me to turn right, that she knew seats were available in the front row. I did as I was told, and she was right! Later, after the show, Allyson stated that Spirit reserved the seats for us. To be honest, I was astonished that no one had taken the seats. I asked people around us if they were reserved for someone, and they said no one claimed the pair of seats.

While watching Sylvia Brown talk about her experiences and give audience members messages about their loved ones that had passed on, I heard in my mind, "Both of you will be doing the same thing in front of large audiences." The message from Spirit was so strong that I told Allyson, "We could do this!" during the event. This was a real turning point in our lives, as we knew that we were destined to be in front of a larger audience.

Allyson contracted to work a Whole Life Expo to give psychic readings at a rented booth and present a talk about 'psychic sense', calling her topic 'Between Two Worlds.' She invited me to join her to work with her. Allyson had already been involved with large holistic fairs and expos, but this was my first large event. I was fascinated by the different groups of people and organizations at the exposition. Helping my sister give readings to people at this show, I was strangely aware of the clamor and how it did not seem to matter, as I was still able to hear from Spirit.

Another nationally-known psychic and author, James van Praagh, was in town as the Whole Life Expo's headliner, presenting a two-hour audience and promoting his current book. I remember there was a huge turnout of people for his talk, as it was the main event amongst the people working at the show. People followed him back to the expo bookstore to buy autographed copies of his latest book.

Whole Life Expo scheduled the 'Between Two Worlds' talk in a smaller lecture room at the expo just after James van Praagh that day. I remember Allyson wondering whether we would have anyone attend our talk, especially after van Praagh. To our surprise, when we opened the doors to the lecture room, I know we were both astonished at how many people filled the room. It was standing room only, with people spilling out of the room. We later figured that the room held roughly 450 people seated and standing. As we began telling the audience our story of how we began at an early age, and relayed messages to the audience, I kept hearing in my head, "This is what you are meant to do." Afterwards, Allyson and I later discussed that this was indeed a turning point in our lives by working with large audiences.

As the talk about 'psychic sense' was going full swing, an expo worker came into the crowded room, interrupting us, stating, "All have to leave now, there is another group needing to use the room for the next hour." The audience had a look of disbelief on their faces, but slowly got up to vacate the room. We told the audience we would be at our booth downstairs to talk to everyone and give readings. Many people waited at the doors of the lecture room as we walked out, wishing to ask questions.

We were stopped quite a few times en route to our booth; many people exclaimed that our talk was much too short. Others approached us, exhorting, "We came to watch James Van Praagh, and that you and Allyson are every bit as good as him!" This was further proof to my sister and me that we were to perform more with large platform groups in the future. The turning point turned; I knew that we were on our way to working on a grand scale in the public.

Allyson—Moving Heaven and Earth through Physical Phenomena

There is materialization phenomena, which has grown for us over the years. Spirit often tries to gain attention by either taking away something in the physical, or to bring objects to Adele or me. As you will see later in this chapter, some items that guides 'borrow' may possibly return, not always returned to the same place. The materialization of objects such as a crystal point, stones, bolts, nuts, coins, feathers, leaves, and flowers have been found inside my houses, cars, even outdoors to be detected. I have discovered feathers inside my house, always white—these were from 'Snowy Owl,' one of my protector guides. I have found United States, Canadian, and South African coins fallen on my welcome mat outside my door, as well as inside the house. I do not collect coins, and those that I receive as 'money from heaven,' especially those that I can use, I spend them! I believe Spirit wants them to be used.

On one occasion I was at the bank waiting at the drive-through, when I heard Spirit say, "Look over here, you will find some dollar bills!" I thought, "No way!" but yes, there they were, twelve dollars lying on the ground next to the bank. It was a windy day in March, and I was surprised to see them lodged in the grass. No one else in line saw them, and I was unsure of getting out of the car to pick up the money. I thought, "Surely, someone dropped this," but after a minute, I got out of the car and picked up the bills. Others noticed what I was doing. A lady rolled down her window to see what I was looking at, and I showed her the rescued money. Another time, I heard spirit tell me I would find seven dollars on the street that I was walking down. Lo and behold, about 25 feet ahead, there were seven one-dollar bills lying next to the gutter of the street. I believe if loved ones in spirit or guides can bring us things, they will move heaven and earth to do this.

I have had fresh green leaves or flowers left in my locked car in the dead of winter! Other times there are stones or unusual items that you will hear fall as if from the height of the room, or fall against a wall or onto the floor, to be found. This is called *apportation*—an item that is brought by spirit is an *apport*, dematerialized from a physical location and carried through the ether to be rematerialized and discovered. In most instances, materialization occurs in an enclosed dark space, such as a room or box. Barbara, a client of mine with mediumistic abilities, had a paycheck dematerialize from a kitchen counter only to find it in her car glove box a week later!

One of the more spectacular cases of rematerialization happened several years ago. Adele gave me a delicate white opal ring for my birthday, and I treasure that piece of jewelry. I made the mistake of taking my rings off, including the white opal, at Adele's house the weekend of July 4th when we had an informal cookout. I placed the rings in my open pocketbook, and should have closed the purse to keep the rings protected. I elected to clean up and wash dishes, and when I finished, I hurriedly picked up my purse and jumped into the car to go home. Four days later, I was looking for my rings, remembering that I left them in the purse. Fortunately, I found my black onyx ring, but there was no opal! I turned the house and car upside-down, but could not find my jewelry. It could have been tossed from my pocketbook. Exasperated, I finally called my twin, Adele, and asked her to look under the nearest pieces of furniture it could have landed. Well, Adele and her husband moved furniture, and nothing turned up. As I laid in bed that evening, she called to give me a negative report. I called out to one of my joy guides, "Daisy, if there is a chance that the white opal ring I lost could be returned, I would sincerely appreciate it coming back, and thank you!" That was the last thought about the ring from that time forward, chastising myself for the way I lost my new ring.

Six weeks later found me teaching classes on Tarot symbolism at Camp Chesterfield in Chesterfield, Indiana. I took care to be spare in baggage, as I had to bring out via automobile my larger teaching materials that took up considerable space. I was also cognizant to bring a dress, which was required for two of the days that I was out there. For those who know Adele and me, we are *not* into dresses, unless it is absolutely mandatory. I made a point of changing pocketbooks, including my wallet to match the purse. I had to look professional!

I stayed at the Western Hotel on the grounds of Camp Chesterfield, and that week it was insufferably humid and hot for August. The first evening I spent at the Camp, I went to the local Wal-Mart and purchased two different size fans. The white noise helped me to sleep at night, but during the first night, I was awakened several times with my travel clock alarm going off by itself. I also awoke the first two nights to what seemed to be bright ectoplasm hovering at the base of the bed, and by a spirit voice that would yell in my ear every hour to 'wake up!' The second night, my frustration of not sleeping forced me to yell out, "Stop this! I need to sleep!" Thereafter I was left in peace. The next morning, I jumped out of bed into the shower, quickly put on clothes to go down to the cafeteria. Grimacing, I remembered that I had vitamins in my coin purse of my wallet, realizing how 'yucky' they get when exposed to humidity. I unzipped the coin purse and turned the wallet upside-down onto the bedspread. Coins, stamps, keys, and a familiar white opal ring fell onto the bed! Believe me, I was in shock! The ring rematerialized inside my coin purse, and now I understand why there had been so much 'racket' during the last two evenings. I shouted out loud, realizing Daisy, my joy guide, brought back the ring to materialize it 700 miles from home, and what a place to bring it to, a camp devoted to mediumship. I directly called my sister Adele, who immediately answered. I could hardly contain myself, I was fairly shouting with joy to tell her that the ring was back. In a class later that morning, I saw Evelyn Reigle, a wonderful medium (deceased as of 2007) who specialized in trumpet phenomena. I handed her the white opal ring, and told her where I found it that morning. Evelyn, in her deep, raspy voice, told the group that her spirits related that the ring had been materialized during the night, and did I notice that there was a color change in the stone? Yes, the white opal now has a greenish cast to the stone overall. This is not unusual if a mineral is dematerialized and then brought back to this world. The chemical structure of the ring is now different, and this is true of many items that are apported. I have the ring back, and it will never be the same.

One evening at an open platform group at my apartment on Gramercy Farm near Baltimore, there was a memorable physical phenomena for those who attended. This involved what looked like 'lightning,' but for those of us there that night, it was a 'sign from Mary.' I am talking about Mary, mother of Jesus, also called Mother Mary.

A picture of Mary hung just behind my reading chair, which is an ornate Savranola post-Gothic piece of furniture handmade for a young Scottish duke, who apparently didn't come of age. The chair has two winged lions with a blank crest on the backrest. The cracked and worn seat is stuffed with horsehair. The arms and legs have hand-carved lions and paws. Suffice it to say that the chair is a great conversation piece.

The platform group moved along with messages for about half of the group present. As I began to speak to one woman, I became aware that I was receiving a message for her from 'Mary,' the same Mary as in the picture above my chair.

I have always believed that it is possible to receive messages from 'higher' spirits other than relatives, and this was one such example. As I related to her that the message was coming from Mother Mary, someone in the room interposed, and I turned to my interrupter on my right. Out of my peripheral vision to my left I saw what appeared to be lightning striking the middle of the room, violently wavering for about 3 seconds. I knew what I saw, and wondered how others reacted to what just transpired! I slowly turned around to look at the group, and clearly half of the gathering on my left observed what happened, due to the response on their faces. The other half of the group beheld nothing at all. When I queried, "Did you all see what happened just now?" The five on the left were in shock, and could barely talk for minutes. One woman was leaning back in her chair, and never did seem to compose herself. It wasn't until she called me a week later, that she related to me something secret. She came to the platform group that night, asking Mother Mary for a 'sign' that she would sell a house that she desperately needed to unload. She related that when I told the other woman that I was 'hearing from Mary,' the lightning arced out of the picture over my chair, over my head, and onto the floor. The 'lightning' did not leave a burn mark, but six of us witnessed that wonder! The house sold in the dead of winter two months later.

Mentioning Barbara's experience above with her missing paycheck has made it clear to Adele and I that when we have worked with clients in groups or audiences as well as in individual readings, there has been physical phenomena associated with our clients in an extended manner. We have seen how psychic ability and physical phenomena will accelerate with some individuals who receive messages from Spirit. Barbara is just one who has seen this happen with her involvement with Adele and me. We have decided to end this chapter to follow with a chapter with several stories given to us by some of our clients. All of them are true.

Allyson—Signs and Wonders

People who know my sister and me have seen unusual and supernatural things happen when we work together. We started noticing this about eleven years ago, before I moved back to the Annapolis area to be near Adele. It began when clients would call me to let me know that their recorded readings on cassette would occasionally not be taped all the way through; others would notify me that static or humming would interfere with the taped readings. I used my own machine about half the time, since many clients did not have recording devices. Several times my Radio Shack recorder would go back for inspection, and always pass 'go,' that is, it was OK. Another early indicator was when Adele and I worked at New Visions Bookstore in York, Pennsylvania for a long weekend. We presented platform mediumship on Friday, and stayed over through Saturday to give readings. This one weekend proved to be interesting in terms of physical phenomena.

Friday night had about 100 people turn out to see us work together. Nothing special about that group, but the following day at the store, many individuals came in and out as it was a normal business day. Bill Trivett, the New Visions Bookstore owner, had floodlights on the ceiling to light his store. As one reading after another was given, Bill noticed that one floodlight after another was blowing out. By noon, three floodlights had already blown. When we had downtime from reading, Bill remarked that something unusual was happening; he asked Adele if this had ever happened to us before. I remarked that there were times that I would have one or two light bulbs blow in one week, but I didn't given it a single thought, because the building I lived on at the Gramercy farm was old and in dire need of rewiring. But this was indeed unusual, to see so many floodlights expire in a commercial establishment. By early afternoon, Adele and I took a lunch break up the street. As we gathered our purses and stepped under floodlights before leaving the store, the lights blew as we walked underneath. In fact, the light arced on a higher level than it illuminated before it blew. Bill, Adele, and I looked at each other in stunned surprise. Bill, incredulously exclaimed, "Don't blow any more floodlights, please! They cost too much!" It was a request in vain, however. Before the day was over, five more floodlights were out, and Bill swore that he now had reason to change his lighting system, which he wanted to do anyway. Today, Bill has a new lighting system in his store, which is filled with high-intensity, small lamps on the ceiling. Since then, none of these lights have blown due our working there.

What clued me in initially with problems with audio and video recording was when I was called and interviewed by a radio station producer from WQXR-FM in Bethesda, Maryland. This was in the spring of 1993, about the time I rented an office on the grounds of Gramercy Farm, a 45-acre organic farm located in Stevenson, outside of Baltimore. It used to be the home of Koinonia, a Christian missionary organization dedicated to teaching young people different trades. Those structures built during the 1960s under Koinonia's tutelage were not of high quality. The electrical systems in all of the buildings were dysfunctional to the point that when I eventually ended up living on the grounds a few months later, after leaving my second marriage with Patrick, I took out renters insurance. I worried about fires there, since there had been a fire on the grounds a few years earlier.

The producer and I came to an agreement over the phone to come to the station two weeks later for a late night talk show program, which would last two hours. Just before ending the phone call, I heard someone in spirit say, "From the frying pan into the fire." I ignored the comment, and proceeded with the engagement when the time came. I took two friends, Richard and Mike, as I was not familiar with the Bethesda area. Since it was a late night show, I wanted male protection, since I didn't know the locale. I intentionally didn't invite my second husband, as he didn't support me in my work. Patrick was a loner; he was jealous of all the attention I received from clients and friends.

When we entered the station, a tall woman approached and welcomed us. Just then, another group of people entered the lobby. Dressed in pretentious black clothing with calf-length coats with hoods, all six announced that they were there for the talk show. The tall woman then asked Richard, Mike and me if we were from the Capitol Skeptics organization, a subscriber-based group who signed on after the producer was told by higher-ups that she couldn't allow me the two-hour show by myself. What would people think? Being normally dressed, I laughed it off. I told the tall woman, the producer from CBS *48 Hours*, that I was the psychic for the evening. Shocked, she quickly looked at the other group, and asked them in an incredulous tone, "And you're the skeptics?" Her look was classic; she had already 'stereotyped' me to look just like the other group! It didn't end there—when we all rode up on the elevator, another person met us, and said virtually the same thing, with the same reaction of shock. I was quickly escorted to the room that I was to work in, and met the radio station DJ producing the show. I was instructed how to work the microphone, and how the show would proceed. The station allowed me to have only one of my male friends to sit in the monitor room with me. I chose Richard, due to his calming influence. I asked Spirit silently to help me with my nervousness while en route to the station. I now asked for the ability to detach myself emotionally from the Skeptics' aggressive attitudes, when I later learned that they were going to create a commotion at the radio station with their group. We were 'on the air' shortly, and I quickly answered questions callers phoned in to the station. We took a break after an hour, and learned that the new talk show, just about had their telephone system crash, because so many people were calling in! I also learned that the Skeptics group brought in a Doctor H, (I won't name names here, to protect his identity) from a paranormal organization on the West Coast. This is what led to CBS *48 Hours'* interest in coming to the radio show to film their "Skeptics" segment. I recognized Dr. H, spoke his name out loud to him, and introduced myself. Dr. H asked me, "How do you know who I am?" I spoke up, "I know that you work with CSICOP." Amazed, he exclaimed, "How did you know that, are you psychic or something?" which brought guffaws by those in the Skeptics organization and the CBS producer. "No," I said softly, "I read." I turned on my heel and went back into the monitor room with the CBS cameraman behind me. It turned out that the television crew traumatized the radio personnel. All seven of the Skeptics group, with Dr. H in tow, pushed their way into the monitor room, and if you could have seen us, we looked like pickled herring in a can! The radio room was too small to hold all of us.

Making this story short, Dr H, with his credentials, found out immediately that he was up against call-in listeners who didn't want to put up with the Skeptic's group point-of-view. Dr. H turned the tables and switched sides. I suppose he realized 'if you can't fight them, join them.' CBS *48 Hours'* producer at the end of the taping asked Dr. H if he thought I was 'credible' as a psychic. "Yes," he stated, "I think she is the real thing."

The CBS *48 Hours* show was slanted to look exactly what the producer wanted viewers of the program to see. The producer 'voiced over' all of my visuals, never allowed me to be voice-recorded on the show. The CBS producer never had me sign a release form. I never knew when the show was scheduled, until it had already aired.

I found out about the program the day after it was on—when I was selected to be on jury duty in Baltimore City. I walked through the Juror's door at the Courthouse and proceeded through the metal detector. A security guard recognized me, grabbed me by my blouse, and pulled me within six inches of his face. "Weren't you on TV last night?" he queried. Fuming, I shook his hand off of me. "Get off of me!" I exclaimed, indignant. "What are you talking about?" In a flash, I understood what it was—the CBS *48 Hours* program! After an hour of listening to jury proceedings, I rushed to the phone and called the local CBS station. After explaining what had happened, the CBS station operator cut me off, saying, "You don't talk to us—you need to call New York, here's the number." With lightning speed, I was speaking to a receptionist in New York, shocked to learn what I had to tell her. CBS didn't want to hear from me, once they realized what had happened. Without a signed release, CBS was legally in the doghouse. I called again, CBS ignored me. Cowards.

I went home shortly; I wasn't selected to be a juror that day. The radio producer at WQXR-FM called. "You won't believe this," she chortled. "From the time that you entered the monitor room until you left the radio program, none of the show taped on the big reel-to-reel recording system, and they're furious upstairs." I realized quickly that spirit had 'done it again.' I started laughing. "Your big 24-hour reel-to-reel cassettes are blank for those two hours? How strange! What do your managers think now of having a psychic on?" She fumbled through her reply; it was obvious 'they' didn't know what to do. They never had me on again!

Another unusual phenomena involved Adele and her home phone. While Adele taught school, she had phone calls from 'the other side' that occur Christmas to New Years' day. The telephone would ring, and in picking up the receiver, Adele would say, "Hello!" and expect that the caller would speak. Instead, a hollow, empty sound on the other end would occur. Sometimes it would be a 'dead' phone, with occasional static. The calls would start on Christmas Day, and there might be two or three of these calls, one after another. She thought someone was dialing their number, playing crank calls. But Adele soon discovered if she needed to make a call after a 'dead' phone, the phone would not work for about ten minutes.

The crazy phone phenomena occurred for several years with a spray of telephone calls that would only take place during the Christmas break. This carried on for about 5 years, until one day Adele answered the phone, to get the dead phone effect again.

Adele spoke into the phone as usual, but this time she said "Hello," and paused, and said it again. In all, she spoke her salutation about five times, each with a pause of approximately 10 seconds. This time, a faraway voice spoke back. If you have ever heard a very bad connection, this was it! Adele relates that a male voice with static interlacing a hollow effect online finally spoke, "Oh, I finally got you!" It was as if a male spirit had been trying for years to somehow telecommunicate and reach across the veil. When Adele finally resolved the 'dead phone' phenomena, and told me about it the day after it happened, it started to happen to me. That same night, the phone would go through the same effects, only Spirit didn't call me during the day. Night after night, from 6PM to early morning hours such as 4AM I would get these calls. After days of being awakened to pick up the phone only to find it dead, I spoke out loud, "Stop this! No more of these calls from you, please." The phone calls stopped altogether. Was this just the workings of one man in spirit, who was trying to contact the living? We never discovered who made these calls.

Allyson—More Signs and Wonders

The preceding chapter illustrates how spirit likes to communicate through mental, auditory, and physical phenomena. Spirit often tells us that any of the above methods can be superimposed upon others to experience. Educating clients on how departed loved ones communicate has many interesting stories relayed to us later, and we think some of these are interesting to our readers, too. All of these are inspiringly factual.

This experience is with the same "Stacey" I wrote about who developed breast cancer. I initially met Stacey in 1997 at one of my 'open' platform groups; she fast became one of my closest friends. We spent many a New Year's Eve together when we had no special boyfriend to be with that holiday. I speak of her now in past tense, as Stacey has now passed over the veil due to the cancer that took her life in October 2006. I miss her deeply as a friend and as a foster daughter. Adele also met her in 1997 at a platform group in an Annapolis bookstore, where Stacey received a message from my twin that she would buy a red sports car. To Stacey's surprise (and dynamic denial!) she did, two years later.

Stacey and I traveled overseas several times to see the avatar, Mother Meera, in Germany. We spent ten wonderful days in Paris staying at the Hilton Hotel overlooking the incredible Eiffel Tower, when Stacey's company held a corporate meeting there. Stacey was a rare happy-go-lucky personality with a compassionate interest in people and her furry feline friends. She worked as a sales representative calling on doctors and made quite an impression on many people, young and old. Because of the nature of her work, she was called in 1999 to work temporarily in New Jersey to learn more about the corporate marketing division. Let Stacey tell the story:

> "Allyson lived in my condominium in Alexandria, Virginia, for seven months, while I worked out of state. Before she moved in, though, we both stood in my living room when she stated, "I think you will be selling this house soon." I didn't

want to hear that! I just bought the condo two years earlier, and I didn't want to think of moving just yet. After settling in New Jersey, our arrangement worked out well, however, every time I came home weird things would happen. In December 1999, I came home for the weekend, and before I dropped my suitcase, Allyson said, "Girl, pack your boxes, you are moving very soon." Two weeks later in New Jersey, I was offered a job in Richmond, Virginia. My company was willing to relocate me. I came home the day before Christmas Eve and hired a realtor to list the house for sale. I questioned Allyson whether the condominium would sell—it was the dead of winter and I wanted to buy another house in Richmond. She resolutely said, yes, that the condo would sell very fast. I remember I came home in early January 2000, for a long weekend. I recall it was the weekend my cousin's twin sons passed away. How devastated Allyson and I were then. The next morning I was by myself putting on makeup in my bathroom, when I heard a rustling in my cosmetic case five feet away from me. I looked around but I didn't see anyone. Allyson came after I called her, and she perceived that the twins' late grandmother, Leah, was in the bathroom with us! Later, I l walked into my garage and smelled roses all around me. I called Allyson again, to see if she dropped a perfume bottle in the garage. (She likes to wear Crabtree and Evelyn's trademark perfume, 'Evelyn'). She replied, "No, why do you ask?" and she soon found out when she walked into the garage. It was hard to believe the garage smelled of roses, when it normally smelled of gasoline and oil from my car. Allyson sharply looked at me and said, "Stacey, you will have a contract on your house today." My realtor called that evening with a contract!

Now that I live farther away, we do not see each other as much as we would like, but we do telephone each other at least twice a month. In December 2003, Allyson called to invite me to spend New Year's Eve with her, which became a tradition for us over the years. I said that I would, even though I now had a boyfriend, but he would be spending the holidays in Baton Rouge, Louisiana. During our phone call, Allyson hesitated, and told me, "Stacey, I need to tell you this—you need to be careful. I see you in bed for a long time." At the time I thought a sinus infection was pending—you know, the kind that takes your voice away, and makes you miserable for two weeks. She advised me to get plenty of sleep and to make sure I ate well. I hate to say it, but Allyson was right again. I drove up to Annapolis, Maryland, on New Year's Eve, and after dinner, we watched fireworks on TV. It was 11:40PM. Allyson uncorked a champagne bottle to celebrate the New Year Ball dropping over

Times Square on television, and we were cracking jokes, laughing hard. I grabbed my sides from laughing too much, and a sharp pain in my chest nearly took my breath away. I panicked, thinking it might be a heart attack. When the pain subsided, I thought, "No, it can't be . . . thirty-five is too young for a heart attack, and besides, there is no pain in my arm." Two or three minutes later, another pain shot across the same area. I grabbed my left breast, held my breath, made a few faces, and finally the pain went away. Well, the fifth pain turned out to be the charm. The pain was so bad that I doubled over, and this time my hand felt a knot in my left breast. I said, "What is this?" I found out several days later through medical screening that the lump was breast cancer—yep, at thirty-five years of age! I was on my back for most of 2004. I am happy to report, however, that we spent New Year's together in 2005 and 2006."

Stacey S. Richmond, Virginia

I wish to include this post-script to Stacey's passing over the veil. I met her stepmother Chickie, and her father, J.T., four months after her passing, and several months later, spent time with her older brother John. Stacey was the 'glue' that held the family together when it was obvious that divorce in the family struck Stacey very deeply. Her parents separated when she was about four years old; she never got over the anxiety of separation from her father. She poured much energy into finding the perfect potential husband, only to have this reality evaporate when men did not live up to her dreams.

After her passing, the pain was so sharp for me that I couldn't feel anything for days. I was not told, nor invited to Stacey's funeral. A friend of a friend relayed the bad news to me twenty-four hours after her death. I was recovering at the time from gallbladder surgery, but had I known, I would have been there for Stacey at her end. After Robin called to tell me about Stacey's death, I immediately shouted out to Heaven, "Stacey, I must hear from you, to know that you are OK up there! You must communicate with me." This demand of mine was insistent; I repeated it over and over the next two days. The evening of the third day, I was relaxing as well as I could on my living room couch, when I distinctly heard Stacey shout out, "Allyson!" Right behind this, I heard two names called out, *Tim*, and *Chris*.

Stacey called out my name in an unusual way, just the way she used to tease me—"All-ee-san." This 'shout-out' was right out of thin air—a 'direct voice,' as it is called by mediums.

The two others names called out were also spoken by two distinct male voices. I knew beyond question then that Stacey found her ability to communicate back to this world. This has not been her only time, though. She made herself visible as she used to appear before she died. I know—she 'visited' me during a platform group near York, Pennsylvania in March, 2007. Stacey did this as an act of love for me and our friendship.

Stacey managed to pull all of her atoms together for approximately five or ten seconds close to the end of the group, for me to see. She appeared somewhat diminutive but *solid-looking*; I know she lost weight from her battle with cancer. Her hair was shorter than I remembered, but other than that, she wore the same clothing I recall her wearing when alive. What I recollect the most was her joy, her aliveness, and happiness to be able to appear in front of the group. Only I was able to see her. She beamed with joy as she pointed to the woman I commenced speaking to, and then she pointed to herself. In my head I heard Stacey say, "Allyson, she has my name." As soon as she stated this, however, her atoms dissolved—my wonderful Stacey was gone! The group noticed the shock on my face; they surmised I had something shocking to tell their friend Cathy. Collecting myself, I managed to relate to everyone present what just transpired, especially Stacey's materialization and message.

Cathy thought about the message and could not relate to either of Stacey's first or middle name. "We don't have either a Stacey or Elisabeth in our family, Allyson." Cathy shrugged her shoulders. I copied her body language, then replied, "Then it has to be her last name, Sprenkle." With this last message, everyone in the room erupted. They either got up or turned in their seat to look at Cathy with surprise. Cathy would not react for a full thirty seconds, then she huffed, "Well, I am no longer married to him, but my daughter still has the last name 'Sprenkle.'" I knew then, without a doubt, that Stacey crossed the hurdle of death to show she knew of no end. I drove home that night from York, Pennsylvania, singing with a wonderful lightness in my being. I related every nuance, every detail of Stacey's apparition to her father several days later when I collected myself. Physical phenomena is real, and everyone can experience it if one believes it.

I met Greg at my home one evening in 2000, when my sister Adele had a rare home-cooked dinner with me. Greg came with his cousin, Doris, another client, not realizing that they showed up the wrong day for the 'open' platform group, held once a month. A tall, strapping, good-natured Italian man in his mid-thirties, Greg is one of those few men that make women secure and happy to be near—he is so comfortable in his own skin. Greg makes women feel like his sisters. Within five minutes, though, Adele and I nailed him about his profession. Able to keep a straight face, Greg would not admit to us what he did for a living, but we knew! I was to hear from a female friend of his three months later—he was freaked out that Adele and I knew where he worked and what he did for a living. He went straightaway to his boss the following morning, and told him whom he had met the previous day. His boss asked for our names and addresses, and said, "I'll be back." His boss came back within an hour, and told Greg, "They're OK." All I can say is that my sister and I are on government files! This is what Greg sent me:

"Allyson possesses and displays an ability that few can comprehend. It has been more than seven years since our first encounter, and I still have difficulty comprehending the breadth of her abilities. It all began for me some years ago when my father (my best friend) was given the news many dread—four weeks to live. Since hospice was unthinkable, I took a leave of absence from work, and cared for him. During his illness, and a few months subsequent to his passing, I experienced a number of things I could not explain within the strict confines of my Catholic faith, or my knowledge of the world as an engineer. Distraught, perplexed and grieving, I assumed I was simply suffering from stress related to the loss of my father, exacerbated by a demanding career with extensive international travel. I knew there had to be more.

A close friend and cousin of my family suggested I read books on metaphysical phenomena. I read authors ranging from the scientists to the faithful, including Gary Zukov, James Van Praagh, Sylvia Brown, John Edwards, and even Tim Allen (yes, Tim the "tool man"). While I grew and became open to the possibility of interaction with a greater existence, it still seemed out of my reach. One day my cousin Doris suggested we visit Allyson Walsh and participate in a group reading with six or seven other folks. Unfortunately, we came the wrong day, but she invited us to stay, and I met her twin sister Adele.

We came back the next week for the group. Just as Allyson commenced with me, I felt a sensation of a hand on my shoulder. Allyson promptly and with apparent ease, began to layout the nature of my employment within the Intelligence community, which is classified. Noting my surprise, she started to identify departed relatives, and conveyed clear and concise messages, the likes of which I had never experienced. She then cited a number of my future travel destinations, many of which I was convinced could not occur, but have since taken place. As she concluded my reading, she glanced back at me, and matter-of-fact added, "That hand on your shoulder . . . it's your father's!"

Confused and emotional, I knew without a doubt that she opened my heart and mind. I've had numerous readings with her and her sister since that night. I often laugh, frequently cry, but I always take notes. Over the years, I have reviewed those notes with amazement. With an uncanny certainty, they have forecast events in my life that I could not fathom at the time. Guidance, reassurance, and love has come from my father and loved ones long since departed from our earthly existence.

Both Allyson and Adele apply their gift with grace and compassion, always mindful of the person, the audience, and the emotions and feelings of those involved. I have asked Allyson to let me stand on the sidelines when they become famous! I want to be there when the rest of the world gets to know them."

Greg C., Germany

I met Carol in 2002 at the Baltimore Womens' Show. Carol was part of an audience when she received a message from her relatives. The message panned out. Carol came to the 2004 Womens' Show in Baltimore to tell us what happened. She stood up to tell the audience her message and its confirmation. Comcast had one of its producers come and film this particular audience, which we have on DVD. Here is her story:

"Dear Allyson and Adele: This is Carol, from the Womens' Show in Baltimore. At the fairgrounds you mentioned that my grandfather Robert and Uncle Johnny came through to warn about an older female in the family needing rescuing in the sense that her health was seriously declining. You said that my relatives in spirit were going to 'rain' coins and coins and coins! I didn't understand the message for some time, but it came true when my reclusive Aunt Jen was found dead by friends on the floor of her house. My brother and I went up to New Jersey to pick up her effects. We walked into the house to find numerous coins stacked in piles all over her house, even on the floor! My brother couldn't believe it when I relayed the message that I received several weeks back, but here it was, coins everywhere! That was your first message. Now, I sat at the second audience two years later, and got another message from Robert and Johnny! My brother received this message through me, and it was that he should look into a baseball camp for men who had wanted to play professionally but didn't . . . WELL . . . I spoke to my brother Sunday. I told him the message from our grandfather and uncle, needing to look into this somewhere in Florida. Long story short, my brother indicated that he was already composing a letter to George Steinbrenner to request that he be allowed to partake in his fantasy baseball camp in Florida! He is not a 'believer.' After he listened to what was needed with the baseball camp, he was taken aback! So much so that he had to end the call to get these facts together in his head. You now have two confirmations that you can tell others. Thanks ever so much . . ."

Carol S., Baltimore, Maryland

Curiously enough, at the date that this book was being written (January 2005), I met a man named Steve F., who runs the Baltimore Orioles fantasy baseball camp! We both met at a local observatory near Glen Rock, Pennsylvania in December 2004. While the local astronomer was busy focusing several telescopes for us, we started talking amongst ourselves, trying to stay warm. Once Steve relayed where he works, I told him about this man who received a message from spirit (I had already told him I was a psychic) about playing in a fantasy baseball game. Steve was open to this, and we hope that Carol's brother went forward with this, after I emailed Carol the news!

This email was received after warming up an audience for Neale Donald Walsch, author of the *Conversations with God* best-seller books. The audience was held Sunday, November 2, 2003, sponsored by my long-time good friend and promoter, Janice Singer R., at the Baltimore BWI Marriott. We were only allowed 30 minutes to talk to the audience before Mr. Walsch went on for his presentation. Adele and I decided to read for two individuals and educate those present about "signs" spirit will present us to let us know they are around. While many were disappointed that we had little time to bring through more messages, we related that loved ones in spirit will bring into the physical world items such as 'pennies' left in obvious places. The following email tells the story:

"Dear Allyson and Adele: I saw you in Baltimore, November 2, 2003. My mother just passed on September 21. I was very close to her and would go to see her several days a week. Even though I talked to her and knew that she was OK, I still needed to hear from her because I had been crying, asking for a sign and prayed to hear from her at the event. I held her picture in my hand, but she did not come through. My sister said, "Mother had other things to do." When I got home I looked on my front steps, hoping to find a penny there, but nothing was there. The next morning I got up to go to work, and when I opened the door, there on the bottom step were three bright, shiny 2003 pennies in the shape of a clover! My mother was Irish and a loyal Eagles football fan. As a matter of fact, her coffin was filled with Eagles trinkets and an Irish tenor sang at her funeral. She also has clovers on her headstone. A friend of mine who went with my sister and me to the Walsch seminar said that the pennies were not there when we left the apartment Sunday morning. My sister has a key to my apartment, but was with me at the event. I thank you and God bless you for telling the audience about 'signs.' I now have a sense of peace and can feel her around me. By the way, the Eagles won yesterday; I guess she was busy with something else!"

Micheline L., Lindenwold, Jersey

The following came from a client who was new to this work. I remember Patti L. came with friends to an August 2002 platform message group; she looked tired, weary from life's experiences. When I have fatigued clients come for readings, especially several in groups, I find that I must call upon one individual in a group to be used for a 'battery,' that is, a person that has more energy to help make up for an exhausted or depleted number of people. In American and British Spiritualist circles, 'batteries' are often used to bolster a medium's energy and amplify the energy of Spirit. Having used 'batteries' before successfully, this was one such evening that it was required!

Patti L. came with the express purpose to hear from her stepfather, Bob. Before beginning the group, I always caution those present that they may come with the expectation of hearing from particular loved ones. Working as an involuntary medium, the expected spirit of a loved one may not come, but someone that he or she knew *will* show up with a message. In this particular reading, her loved one Bob did come through, but was giving her all kinds of physical phenomena to let her know that he was 'there' for her. She needed me, the medium, to point this out to her:

"Dear Allyson: I came to see you in late summer of 2002. I was in the middle of a lot of stress because of getting my widowed mother moved to Virginia from North Carolina. I had hopes of hearing from her husband, my stepfather Bob, whom

I loved dearly, and who had passed away less than 2 years prior to this date. I had been praying and asking for his help in this transition for my mother.

I was surprised by the fact that my mother's mother was the first to come through. I had never known this woman, as she passed when I was a very small child. In any case, she knew about my mother's declining health, said she was watching and was concerned about her. She sent her encouragement to me to get my mother moved to Virginia as quickly as possible, as she would continue to decline in health if we did not. She assured me that my mother would appreciate what was done for her, but after the move to Virginia, her health would improve. Let me add here that we did make the move for my mother. Even though we had some trials, she is doing well, although she still terribly misses her husband, Bob.

At that point, Allyson mentioned male names like Robert, Ronald. I said I didn't know anyone by that name that had passed, but had a brother named Robert and one named Ronald. Then Allyson mentioned she smelled smoke and this person she felt was very relaxed. Well! I immediately broke into tears and yelled, "Bob!" Bob was a heavy smoker and probably the most relaxed and optimistic person I knew! I forgot that spirits can come through using their proper name, and I guess I was so anxious to hear from Bob, that I just didn't make the connection immediately when Allyson said the name 'Robert,' his given name. He said that he appreciated me talking to him, that he 'hears' me. He asked me to light a candle for him. Allyson interjected here that if we light candles for those on the other side, and send positive thoughts and love to those on the other side, it creates a stronger bond, and gives 'strength' to spirit to move higher into the astral world. He sent his love to me and assured me that he was there for me as well.

Bob mentioned that he had been trying to get my attention with 'lights' or a blinking light. A friend who was with me laughed and said that wasn't going to work in my house, as my husband is an electrician and he would immediately fix any light he thought there was something wrong with. We all got a big kick out of that! A few days later when I returned to work, Bob got his chance to get my attention. I absolutely hate fluorescent lighting (as do my co-workers), so we keep lamps in our office space. I was in the office by myself that following Monday after my reading. As I stood at my desk, something 'told' me to turn toward my co-worker's desk across the way, and I did. She was not in yet, and all her lights were turned off. As I turned to look, her top bookshelf lamp blinked on and off three distinct times—not like a bulb flickers when it is loose or going out, but three, slow and deliberate times it went on and off again. I smiled and felt such a sense of comfort, knowing Bob was there with me. It doesn't stop there! I had already been in my boss' office, where I never turn on her lights (I let her do it when she comes in). I forgot to take something into her office and when I went back, I found that the overhead fluorescent light was on. Okay, I didn't turn it on, so who did? I was sure it was Bob and again, I felt a pure sense of peace.

There have been a few times since then that he has played with the lights at my workplace and I always just smile, welcome him, say hello, etc. Funny, he doesn't do it at the house too often—perhaps he does know that my husband will just try to fix them!

To this day, I light a candle for Bob. Sometimes I forget, so I don't do it every night, but I do several times a week. I feel it keeps a strong bond between us. Although I miss him terribly still (like my mother does), I know he is safe and happy, and I will see him again one day. And, I'd like to thank Allyson for making that connection for me. It sure helps the spirit—both mine and his!"

Patti L., College Park, M D

Sometimes our clients do not understand a message given in a reading until they return home, and physical phenomena will spark the event of knowledge. I received a client, Sharon A., in the summer of 2005, along with her friend Richard, to which she told me the following:

"I visited Allyson for the first time in March 2004, nine months after my mother died. Allyson knew immediately that my mother had passed. She brought her in, and told me that 'peace roses' were all around my mother. I didn't know what peace roses were at that time. My mother never liked flowers, as she had emphysema and couldn't tolerate the smell. I didn't understand the reference. Allyson told me it would make sense later. And it did, the next morning.

The next morning while I was showering, I heard something crash in the tub with me. I looked down and saw a small hard plastic vase with artificial multi-color roses. That vase had been in that location for several months, and never fell before. I think that was my mother trying to let me know that she is around me. It was extremely comforting to me. I am so thankful to Allyson for making me understand that."

Sharon A., Washington, D.C.

Sometimes clients receive messages that seem unbelievable to them, like the message from "Mary," a recently deceased grandmother to skeptical Lori. Lori always appeared stressed the few times I saw her; many of her troubles were based on issues concerning her divorce and custody issues with her two children. The message she received from her grandmother was hard for her to believe, especially when Family Court is reluctant to bend to a mother's interest. Imagine my surprise when I receive this email from Lori several months later:

"I want you to know that I participated in a platform reading August 2005, that was held at my Aunt's house in Colonial Beach, Virginia. During my reading, Allyson received a message from my recently departed grandmother, Mary, that I would win an upcoming legal hearing. As excited and hopeful as I was to hear this spirit communication, deep inside, my hope had dissipated. I was advised repeatedly by three separate attorneys that I would not win my legal battle to change my daughter's last name to the last name that belonged to both me and her brother. There have not been many cases that have been successful in the Court's history. The burden of proof was on me to convince the judge that this decision would be in my daughter's best interest.

Nervous and still hopeful, on the morning of September 15, 2005, I continued to talk to my grandmother Mary before and during the Court hearing, asking her to be with me during my difficult testimony and cross-examination. It was like a dream when I heard the judge rule in favor of my request. The judge stated that my case was unique in nature and he was satisfied that I fulfilled my obligation of presenting sufficient evidence.

It was at that precise moment of the ruling that I *again* received affirmation from the other side that my grandmother was with me, and that she was continuing to watch over my children."

Lori R., Washington, D.C.

Even Edie, my cleaning lady, is not immune to things happening. Shortly after starting to clean my home one Monday morning in 2005, the television in the living room was turning on and off as Edie stood nearby. She came back to my office, leaned in and yelled above the vacuum cleaner, "Allyson, come out here and see what's happening to your TV!" Jumping out of my office chair, I stared blankly as the television flipped on and off. Picking up the remote, the television refused to obey commands from the remote, so I unplugged the TV for a while. I know that Edie was spooked, so to speak, and later on in the afternoon I replugged the television, and it worked fine.

Edie came to me several months later, and wanted me to read for her. I sat her down in my office; energy liked to a whirlwind or tornado was spinning from her feet up to her throat area. I knew that based on that type of energy that many things were changing in her life. This type of energy generally looks like chaos, or the leading edge of change, which is generally good. As we finished her reading, I mentioned her father by name coming through in spirit and told her, "Your father is looking to contact you by telephone!" Edie looked at me, not knowing how to react to this statement.

Several hours later, I receive a voicemail on my telephone. It goes like this:

> "I want you to know that I didn't believe what you said about my Dad, who passed two years ago, coming through to say that he was working on contacting me by phone. Imagine my shock when I got home and out of habit, I checked caller ID. There was my father's old office number! Let me explain that I have had no contact with employees from this office since my father's death. The time of the call was from after business hours!

This email came to me just as I was ready to send this manuscript off to the publisher. I decided to include it because it happened at the Christmas 2007 season for a elder mother and a female client named Shirley. The physical phenomena which occurred after a reading for Shirley several weeks earlier inspired her to let us know what transpired.

> "Hi Allyson and Adele: You wanted to know what happened with Uncle Joe, who has come through in your reading for me. My Mom visits here every Christmas from Upper Michigan for a month or two to get away from the harsh weather in Calumet. It snows most of the winter and she doesn't get out much. She looks forward to coming here and I enjoy having her. At your platform message session you told

me 'Joe' was present. You told me Joe has a sense of humor and that he was going to play a trick with my Christmas tree ornaments.

I went home and explained to Mom, "Your brother Joe came to visit tonight and is supposed to play a trick with the Christmas tree." Unbelieving, Mom just went along with the story. We both looked at the Christmas tree which was about four feet away from the sofa and noticed that one ornament at a time swaying slowly. They moved one at a time in different areas on the tree, randomly, not like a draft blew and moved them all. At one time at least 15 were moving. Mom got up and slowly moved to the tree in awe. There was a ball in the back of the tree, and she said, "Look, this red one is moving too." Slowly, then, they stopped moving. I sat motionless thanking Joe for visiting us. They started moving again! There weren't as many moving this time and gradually, it came down to only one crystal star at the top of the tree beneath the angel tree topper that was the last one to stop its movement. It took about a half an hour for this episode to conclude. I wanted to get my movie camera but was afraid to move away and miss something. It was a very personal moment for both of us. I felt softness in my heart that Uncle Joe was looking over us. He was a kind, gentle person, who taught me more than I ever realized. He lived with us growing up, as my father had left before I was born. My mother and sisters were allowed to living with my single uncle Joe in my grandfather's house as long as my mother didn't marry. He died of stomach/colon cancer when I was seventeen years of age. I will always think of him as my 'little crystal star under an angel' who watches over us."

Shirley Z, Glen Burnie, Maryland

Allyson—A Change of Mind

The following story illustrates how someone can display strong belief in their own convictions about life, yet have no idea of what waits for them when they cross over. Lily, in the next story, had to endure a father who demanded all of his children to believe 'one way, or it's the highway.' Unfortunately, this caused a major riff between Lily and her dad. Lily's father Joe, however, has not been one to be deterred in being heard from once he crossed, as you will read:

"Dear Allyson and Adele: I attended the Thursday, May 27, 2004 audience advertised at the Holiday Inn in Baltimore, Maryland, hoping very much that I would get messages. At that time, my father was terminally ill with cancer and I sensed that he did not have very long to live. I longed to comfort my beleaguered father before he passed, but because he believed that when "you die, that is it," I had no avenue to change his mind about what to expect when he crossed. My father never supported my beliefs; often he would not let me in to see him at home or in the hospital.

Three days before the audience I had a dream that I was encased in a rose quartz-colored bubble. I associate rose quartz with love. In this dream there was a cabin in deep woods. I walked towards the cabin; a woman with beautiful long hair dressed in a white gossamer dress opened the door to greet me. There was something vaguely familiar about the woman but I did not recognize her. She assured me that everything would be all right. A white Pegasus-like creature walked up to us. The woman walked out of her doorway towards him to pat the creature as she introduced him to me. His given name was "White Elk". She claimed that White Elk was there to help her take care of things. Later, I realized that this lady was my paternal grandmother, Rosa . . . younger than I had ever seen her in life.

During the platform group, Allyson and Adele gave many messages from Joes, Roses, and Rosettes. Joe was my paternal grandfather's name and Rosa was my paternal grandmother's name (both now crossed over). I held a key ring with a rose etched inside a lucite rectangle. I hoped to hear from my grandmother or grandfather—I had been praying, beseeching many loved ones to help my father make a smooth transition. In life he shunned my being a Spiritualist and basically washed his hands of me. When for the third time Allyson said she had another Joe in spirit I spoke up saying that I thought it was for me . . . Allyson said that it was not for me—she would come to me later.

After a while, Allyson clutched her right side and said that there was someone present in the audience that had a liver operation. I was shocked; I had been discharged from the hospital a week earlier after having liver surgery; in fact, I still had 23 staples in my incision. Allyson next said she had Lillie, my beloved maternal grandmother who always comes through for me, and William Theodore, my uncle. She then related that she had a Charles who said that he and my father were close, like brothers. I thanked them all for coming, and appealed to them to help my father transition, so that he would not be alone or get lost between worlds. My grandmother Lillie said, "Hello!" to pass on to her daughter for her.

The next day, I went to visit my mother. We spoke on the porch outside because my father would not allow us to talk about Spirit and messages in his presence. I reassured her that her mother Lillie would be there for Dad and for herself as well. I also spoke about Charles. My mother said that she had just received a letter from her friend, Juanita, who had been married to Charles. In the letter, Juanita stated my father and Charles were like brothers. My mother believes in messages most of the time but it also frightens her. My mother's birthday is May 19. My brother sent her a flower arrangement with pink roses, stargazer lilies, and carnations. Most of the flowers had dried up except for two stargazer lilies that opened several days after the arrangement arrived. My father's cap was on the table next to the flowers and lying, pressed in the middle of his cap, were the fresh petals of a stargazer lily that had just bloomed. I saw this and told my mother that grandmother Lillie picked that fresh bloom and put it on dad's cap to prove to her that her message was real . . . my mother looked at it and said, "it's a miracle." Three days later, May 30th, my father passed away.

On the morning of June 4, 2004 we were getting ready for my father's funeral. I went downstairs to the laundry room to press my suit. My mother was undecided as to what to wear with her dress. The dress came with a three-quarter-length jacket.

My mother tried on the black jacket and it fit well. I took the jacket downstairs to press, but the iron that I had just used would NOT work. My mother had another iron, so I plugged it in and it, too, would not work. I suddenly felt a cold chill; the hairs on my arms, neck and the crown of my head stood up. I heard my father say, "Not black, do not mourn!" I raced up the stairs to tell my mother that I had just heard from Dad—that he did not want her to wear all black and mourn. Since then, I have used the iron and it works just fine.

Hoping to hear again from my father, I traveled to Tranquil Waters Bookstore on June 10, 2004. After a while, Allyson turned to me to give me messages. Allyson had a 'Joe' come through, claiming he had not gone 'home' yet, wearing a fedora-style hat. He said he passed about two weeks ago. "That is my Dad . . . he passed May 30th . . . ten days ago!" I exclaimed. Joe said he was now thrilled that I am involved in this metaphysical interest. All of a sudden Allyson grasped her chest, claiming her heart was flip-flopping. Joe was making her feel very sad and remorseful. Joe's message to me was, "I'm so sorry, I am very proud of your work . . . in life I was hard-hearted and hard-headed." Allyson, with tears streaming down her face, related what he said next, "I threw up my hands with you." My uncle 'William Theodore' came through next to say hello. Allyson spoke of a 'Rosa' (my paternal grandmother who was in my dream two weeks earlier), and my beloved 'Lillie' (my maternal grandmother) came through. Allyson imitated her gesture. She grasped the top of each side of her shirt, pulling it forward in a proud, boastful manner. This indicated to me that my Lillie was proud to answer my pleading prayers to greet my dad and be with him during his transition. My father then came through to say hello to 'Marlene' (my mother). My friend 'Glynnis' came forward next with the message that she was here to 'buck me up' and she sent 'lots of love.' My cousin 'Gladys' came through next. Lastly, my joy guide named 'Singing Lilly' said hello and goodbye!

After the platform group, I asked Allyson if she would like to go out to get a bite to eat. My siblings often tease our mother telling her that at night her house is 'locked down' like Fort Knox. In the middle of our meal Allyson pulled out her mobile phone from her purse and said, "Spirit just told me to tell you to call Marlene." I called my mother, Marlene—she was up waiting for me so that she could lock the house down.

After arriving home while reflecting over the evening events I noticed that there were twenty-two saved messages on the answering machine. Earlier that day, four times the phone rang and no one said anything. I told my mother that Dad was trying to call us. My mother does not know how to erase old messages so I decided to do it for her. After erasing a few messages I came to a message that was a man's voice, almost in a whisper, and the message was breathed, "Okay". I listened to the message again and it clearly was my father letting us know he was okay. My mother heard the message, too.

On June 17, 2004 I went with Allyson to New Visions Bookstore in Pennsylvania. I was not expecting to receive a message, I just wanted to hang out with my friend. Allyson started reading for a man and suddenly my father interrupted his reading by jumping in front of the spirit that Allyson was attending. He was so happy to be able to communicate! He had with him a man in uniform, who had many medals and was friends with many lawmen—it was 'Sarge,' my father's best friend who passed away in 1979. I used to jokingly call Sarge 'Numbers' . . . because before there was a legal lottery, there was an illegal numbers racket that Sarge ran. Sarge was protected by many policemen. I sent thoughts to my father and Sarge, asking, "Send me winning lottery numbers!" My father's message to me was, "There is so much here to see, and I am with you." He also sent love to my mother. Allyson then said there was also a man with my father named 'Ron.' I did not know who he was. I later asked my mother who was Ron and she also did not know.

On my way home from New Visions Book Store I stopped by the local 7-Eleven to call my mother to unlock the doors so that I could get in the house. I got in my car and started backing out of the parking space. As I looked back, I saw a sign on a pole that read 'Lottery Is Back.' I pulled back in the parking space, went inside the store and purchased a scratch-off ticket. Just before going to bed I remembered the ticket and started scratching. I won one hundred dollars! Thank you Dad and Sarge!

I called Allyson immediately to tell her of my winning ticket. Allyson had a question for me—she asked me "what is a 'numbers racket?' Apparently my father and Sarge were still talking to her when she drove home from York, Pennsylvania.

Thursday morning, June 16, 2004, I called my mother. She asked if I was sitting down—I said yes. Mother said, "Your father called this morning . . . it was your father . . . he spoke only one word, just 'David'." David, my youngest brother, came later that evening to spend the night and tend our mother. David took her the following day to Lancaster, Pennsylvania to see the musical 'Noah.'

On Saturday, June 26, 2004, I was sitting on the sofa in my mother's family room when I saw a page torn loose from a small address book on the table, peeping out from a pile of mail. I recognized my father's handwriting. I looked through the pile and found the rest of the book. I wondered if I would see a "Ron" in my father's address book. I started at the beginning; when I got to the G's there was 'RON Gentry!' I went to the kitchen to tell my mother what I had found . . . she exclaimed, "I never knew Gentry's first name. He was a good friend that worked with your father . . . I met him only once."

Thank you Allyson and Adele for allowing God to work through you . . . because of your love of God and doing His work you have helped me and my family immeasurably.

Lorraine F., Baltimore, MD

Allyson—The Civil War and Its Ghosts

The summer of 2004 proved to be busy and fruitful. Several clients from U.S. Foodservice organized a 'girl getaway,' asking me to lead some platform groups with a twist. As we gals stayed at the Cashtown Inn, Cindy and Debbie wanted me to conduct platform message circles along with touring some of the more famous battlegrounds and shops around Gettysburg, Pennsylvania. The bustling town of Gettysburg is full of tourists wanting to experience everything from re-enactments to ghost tours. While I toured the battlefield years ago in my high school days, I never felt the urge to go to Gettysburg until Debbie and Cindy asked if I would like to go with them. Since then I have led tours of Little Round Top, the Evergreen Cemetery Gatehouse (where President Lincoln delivered his famous Gettysburg Address), Cashtown Inn (where General Lee's troops moved through Cashtown, en route to Gettysburg), Lightner Farmhouse (which was used as a Union hospital), the Farnsworth Inn, and several ghost tours of the Jennie Wade House, which the Travel Channel considers one of their top 10 most haunted houses.

In 2005, it was while I was en route to Gettysburg from Reisterstown, Maryland, that I may have had one of my more unusual experiences, of which I had absolutely no control. Spirit, namely one named 'Joe,' decided to use me as an instrument to deliver a message to a niece, whom I did not know.

I had just left a sumptuous Indian buffet restaurant on Reisterstown Road and was headed due north to pick up Route 140 to Westminster, Maryland. I followed a bakery truck with a very large graphic advertisement on the back end illustrated 'Thomas' English Muffins'™ most of the way through Westminster. The name 'Thomas' stood out in such a way that only spirit makes possible when spirit wants to—and I made a comment to myself, "The name 'Thomas' is going to mean something to someone at the Lightner Farmhouse tonight." I was to meet Deb and Cindy with ten other participants of our Gettysburg weekend. I made a mental note to try to remember the name 'Thomas.'

The trip was uneventful until I got through Westminster. Route 97 is a delightful road to travel, with old houses and lots of farmland to appreciate. As I drove the two-way road up into the hills past the Mason-Dixon division line of Maryland/Pennsylvania, I heard clearly in my head that I needed to 'go to a floral shop.' Not once, but three times! I kept driving, wondering why would I want to go to a florist? I was sure that the Lightner Farmhouse would have all the flowers they need, so I stopped thinking about it. I soon hit the town of Littlestown, quaint but in need of rejuvenation. Again I heard, "Stop at the florist shop!" Almost right on top of a sign that said 'Florist,' I jerked the steering wheel sharply into the driveway. I almost overshot the driveway, which took me behind the house to park. Turning off the ignition, I got out of the car, wondering what in the world was I doing there. I noticed a woman intently looking at something on the back stoop of the house, and wondered if I was intruding here. I called out, anxiously, "Do I go to the front of the house for the shop?" I looked at the vehicles next to my car; they were indeed flower delivery vehicles.

"Sure, yes, go to the front of the building." I tentatively ventured around the house, and saw two entries. I climbed the stairs of the first, grabbed the door, and for a moment, I stepped back down, still not sure of what I was doing there. I felt magnetized to go back to the door and went in.

Walking around the small rooms filled with candles, silk flowers, and knickknacks, I waited to see if something would stand out for me to notice why I was there. Some candles were nice, and I considered buying them, but I waited a little longer. Janet, a blonde woman in her forties who was out back on the stoop, now approached me with a query if I needed help. Exasperated, I told her I didn't know why I was here, that I was on my way up to the Lightner Farmhouse, six miles past Littlestown. I told the lady that I was going to work with twelve people who wanted to experience ghosts and mediumship, which was my specialty as a professional psychic. Janet's eyes widened, and with a grin she spoke appreciatively of local psychics and of John Edwards and James Van Praagh. I explained that I worked in a similar manner to John Edwards. Janet told me that a local psychic named Paul told her many things that came true.

As I listened to Janet speak, I heard in my head the names, "John, and Joe." A terrible feeling came over me about her father; I knew he was seriously ill. I felt that he did not have long to live. "Janet," I explained, "I must tell you that I hear the names 'John' and 'Joe' to you. You know who they are."

"Why yes, I do. John is my Dad, and Joe was his brother, my uncle, now gone. How did you know this?" she asked.

A moment passed before I felt confident enough to relay the message. Janet would be able to hear the reason that Spirit pulled me off the road, walk into a stranger's business to give her a message from the Divine. "Janet, I don't like giving these kind of messages, but I believe Joe knew that you will be all right to hear this—your Dad is not going to live long past August of this year, so enjoy him as long as you can." I have to admit I was in awe of this Joe, needing to pass a condolence message to his living niece. The only way he could do it was to find a human telephone, driving up the road past her business.

It turned out Janet was receptive to hearing the unfortunate news. She already knew from her psychic Paul and two medical doctors that her father, John, was not long for this world. I picked up two of the candles I eyed earlier to purchase, and Janet and I talked about mediumship for a while longer. She asked for my business card, and Janet handed me one of hers. When I saw her last name, I exclaimed, "So you are 'Thomas!' I followed a bakery truck in Reisterstown with a graphic on the back for 'Thomas's English muffins'™, and knew that somewhere, someone needed a message with the name 'Thomas!' And here you are!" It was now tied together, the whole shooting match. Joe managed a nice job of providing enough information to surprise both his niece and myself. I am certain if he could pull off that trick, that Janet may have some physical phenomena occur at a later date with her relatives on the other side.

July Fourth of 2005 also proved to be interesting as my friend and student Ally H. took me to see the Wayside Inn in Middletown, Virginia. Ally knew that I wanted to meet a man named Leo Bernstein, who owns the Wayside Inn, along with many of the Museums in Strasburg, Virginia. For me, it was the Jeane Dixon Museum I long wanted to tour since it opened in March 2003. We hoped to find Leo Bernstein at the Wayside Inn, but no one was sure if he was in Virginia or in Georgetown (District of Columbia), visiting his wife. It was, in fact, a holiday.

For those that read this and do not know who Jeane Dixon was, she was the world-famous psychic from Washington, D.C. who warned President John F. Kennedy's secretary to not have the President go to Texas in 1962. She received her psychic impression strongly in a cathedral in Washington, D.C., that the President would be assassinated. Ruth Montgomery wrote a book about Jeane Dixon, which catapulted her to notoriety thereafter.

Leo Bernstein was Jeane Dixon's banker in D.C. for many years before she died in 1997. He inherited many of her belongings, including her famous crystal balls. I have heard Ally tell me several times that she felt that Leo was psychic himself. When she met him several years ago, he held her right hand, and told her intimate things he could not know. When asked about Leo's psychic side, the manager on duty at the Wayside Inn, Paul, didn't know anything of the sort.

Ally and I were joined by one of her friends for lunch, and we weren't disappointed by our fare. Our waitress, Dorothy, was quite accommodating, and mentioned that the Wayside Inn was haunted, after we ventured to tell her that we saw the chandelier swinging above us. It seemed that someone was 'rocking' in a rocking chair just above us as well, because we could hear it. *Was someone staying in the room?* We asked Dorothy, and she said she would find out. Moments later, Dorothy reappeared, and stated matter-of-factly that no one stayed in that room in the inn overnight, it was 'clean.' Ally declared resolutely, "Surely a ghost must be upstairs rocking, we heard so much noise above us! Would it be possible for us to see some of the Inn?" Dorothy left to obtain permission to see if we could visit the Inn in a way unknown to most visitors!

Dorothy returned, and stated that we could see several rooms known to be haunted. She spoke of seeing a little girl with blonde ringlet curls when she first started working at the Wayside Inn. The child looked to be about five or six years of age, and was known by the staff to be 'mischievous.' Things were seen to float through rooms, voices called out, and belongings were often moved. As Dorothy spoke, I heard the name 'Sarah' several times. I spoke up. "Dorothy, do you know anyone in spirit here as 'Sarah?' She shook her head no, but she could find out if the staff knew. They apparently kept registration books of early known visitors of the Inn.

Finishing lunch, Dorothy took us to the rooms known to have ghosts frequently. The first room was the 'Little Girl's Room,' known by staff where guests move out to other quarters occasionally, as the 'little ghost-girl' didn't always like her room's occupants! As we moved into the bedroom, I immediately was drawn to the two drawings of the child next to the closet. Dorothy stated, "These are pictures of the little girl. She looks just like these." I peered closely to the small type under the lead drawing. It said, 'Little Sarah.' I spoke it out loud, not realizing I did. Ally shot back, "What did you say?" I said, 'Little Sarah!'" I looked directly at Dorothy, and asked,

"Did you know that this picture had a name under it? This must be your ghost!" Dorothy genuflected for a moment, and declared, "No, I never noticed that before. It looks like we know who she is now!" With this, we moved on to other rooms. I was intrigued with the 'Lincoln Room,' where Jeane Dixon often stayed when she visited with Leo Bernstein. I also appreciated some of Jeane's memorabilia that Leo has in a hallway.

Soon thereafter, we stopped at the desk, and inquired if they knew if the Jeane Dixon Museum was open. Paul, the manager on duty, telephoned the museum, and told us, yes, it was open. Before leaving, Paul spoke to me. "Would you be willing to work here in the off-months entertaining guests about the Inn and reading people here?" I looked at him in amazement. I am already doing this in Gettysburg, and said so. I am sure Dorothy ran back and told the staff what happened when she left us upstairs to look at the Lincoln Room!

I cannot recall another incident where an individual awoke me from a dream to get out of bed to do something! I was deep in a dream March 28, 2006, hearing myself sing along with others at a packed concert. The country band and male singer was unknown to me consciously. I felt pulled to 'get up' and write down the words of the stanzas coming to me in my head. Fortunately, I had left my computer on overnight; the lyrics of four stanzas poured out. Aware that I felt two spirit men standing behind me, I realized that 'they' were the cause of the music—I have never had the volition to write music composition as I am stymied by how music notation worked. I was aware of their names—I heard the name 'Davis' first, but did not know whether that was a first or last name. I doodled the name 'Key' on a notepad, along with the words, 'national anthem,' but as I was tired, I wasn't thinking. At that hour I could not have told you what the national anthem was. I had the good sense to find a cassette tape and record the melody into my tape recorder before I became too sleepy to continue. It was six in the morning when I went back to bed.

The next morning, again at 6AM, with the morning sun shining through the trees into my office, I heard the transitional piece, which I added. Three mornings later, on April 1st, I was awakened, same time, with what I was told was to be two more stanzas to the patriotic musical piece.

Here is where it gets strange. With the initial music written on March 28th, I had a client coming to see me later that day. Have you ever had a melody get 'stuck' in your head? It was all I could hear that day, that patriotic song. Dottee H. showed up for her reading later that afternoon; 'Davis' spoke up during her reading, which shocked me. He wanted me to sing the song to her. This I did not want to do! I asked Dottee, "Do you know a relative in your family passed by the name of 'Davis, and would you mind if I sing a small piece of a song that came to me this morning?'" Dottee assented, and after hearing the music, asked, "What does he look like to you?" I replied, "Well, he wears an out-of-date uniform. His hat has something like guns crossed above the brim. Do you know who he is?" Dottee looked at me very serenely, and said, "Yes, you are bringing in my great, great, great, great, great-grand-uncle, Jefferson Davis—the President of the Confederacy during the Civil War." I was stunned; never has anyone from so far back come through. I showed her the notepad where I scratched the words 'Key,' and 'national anthem.' Dottee added, "You must have had Francis Scott Key, along with my great grand-uncle Jefferson Davis, visit you this morning. It sounds like they inspired you to write these lyrics. Times are hard right now for our country being so divided over the war in Iraq. It seems that Davis and Key want to help bring our country together—what better way than through music?" I couldn't have agreed more. I decided to include the lyrics here in the book for all to see. Perhaps someday we will have a singer worthy enough to record this.

How Great You are!

From fruited plains to majestic mountains,
Shining seas to darkening skies,
The dreams of "We the People,"
Awake to others' cries.
Terror gripping the nation
Looming battlefronts give signs.
USA—How great you are!

From Revolution to the present,
Our freedom's been on the line.
We've worked hard to be a nation,
Betsy Ross was so inclined.
We've dug deep to get together
911 was unkind.
USA—How great you are!

In the past, our wars were clear-cut,
We rallied around the flag.
From California to Fort McHenry
We couldn't let our spirits sag.
When the boots of Heaven trample,
God's wrath flying through the mag.
USA—How wonderful you are!

Now young men are on the front lines,
Helping others see the need.
Freedom's call to other countries
The enslaved want to be freed.
Helping those that are in danger,
Become like us, a rare breed.
USA—They will see how great you are!

Rockets flying through the red air,
Angels! Please defend our men!
Overdue the call to justice,
We call upon our friends.
Hard is the cry for freedom,
The enslaved want God's amends.
USA—They will know how great you are!

Time's felled the walls for justice,
Making freedom ring for others.
No longer nation against nation,
Pulling altogether as brothers,
Knowing now this precious freedom,
God's grace upon your shoulders.
USA! You will know how great you are!

More Ghosts and Spirit Emanations

My sister Adele may throw a fit when she realizes this manuscript was ready to go to the publisher when it became clear that Spirit wanted me to include this chapter. I realized that we needed to include our Cashtown Inn investigation that we did with the P.E.E.R. ghost-hunting group in Cashtown, Pennsylvania, on November 4, 2007. Adele and I were invited by Steve McNaughton, whom, along with his wife, Tina, owns the 'Chestnut Hall Bed &Breakfast,' one of the most charming bed and breakfasts right outside of Gettysburg, in New Oxford, Pennsylvania. Their inn has its resident ghosts, albeit they are primarily little children who visit and play in the graceful Queen Anne house now and then, along with a cat in spirit that leaves these owners little deceased critters in plain view for them to find! New Oxford is considered the 'antique capital' of Pennsylvania. Besides our interests in things metaphysical, Adele and I share an interest in 'things antique.' As the PEER group was looking for a 'sensitive' or medium to help in their investigation, Steve McNaughton suggested us to the ghost-hunting group to look at the Cashtown Inn.

The red brick Cashtown Inn was constructed in 1797 to be the first stage coach stop west of Gettysburg. As Cashtown is only 9 miles from Gettysburg, the inn was used primarily as the Confederate Army's headquarters and as a hospital. Historians claim that more Confederate soldiers passed through the front door of the Cashtown Inn than any other building north of Richmond. General A.P. Hill moved 22,000 soldiers in and around Cashtown. It is a wonder that the tiny town could manage hospitality for that many people. General Lee met with General Hill here, passing through town July 1, 1863. It was General John Imboden that transferred the wounded to the Cashtown Inn after the evacuation of the Gettysburg Battle on July 4, 1863. All of the above information Adele and I garnered after our walk-through.

November 4, 2007 found us outside the Cashtown Inn around 8PM with about 15 ghost-hunters. We were exceedingly lucky to have Steve McNaughton get permission for all of us to tour the Inn; however, only my sister Adele, Steve, myself, and Jim Zero were allowed upstairs on the second and third floor for the first 90 minutes. The owner of the Cashtown Inn graciously closed the whole Inn down that night; there were no visitors, no diners, nor overnighters in order for us to look for ghosts. The bartender who stayed with us in the hotel that evening impressed upon us the fact that the Inn lost several thousand dollars that night in order for us to do this hunt.

The Pennsylvania ghost-hunting group asked to get our impressions of the place—namely, they wanted to see if we could bring through names of anyone there in spirit. As my interest in the Cashtown Inn came through a different route, namely a few years earlier with a 'girl getaway' (see chapter entitled, 'The Civil War and Its Ghosts') with no real interest in Civil War history, I wasn't so sure we would get anything. In fact, as we moved into the front room with its hallway that leads to the restaurant, I knew I was nervous.

Both Adele and I were hit with nausea almost as soon as we walked into the front room. I looked up the staircase, somewhat anxiously. I recall with the 'girl getaway' of 2004 that all of us gals, about nine of us from New Jersey and Baltimore, were more interested in what the local shops of Gettysburg inspired us to buy than its historical information. Unbeknownst to me, these gals decided I had to stay in the most haunted room in the Inn, but were perplexed when our two-night stay had everyone else terrified at night when spirits sat on them or made enough noise to keep them up at night! (My own people in Spirit usually keep others away, but not always). We gals sat in that front room (what is considered the 'lobby' today) the first evening, telling ghost stories, and I intuitively instructed everyone with digital cameras where to shoot in the room to catch ghosts on film. Barbara Roberts' daughter, Emily Grace Freed, took the advice and shot a picture of the lobby staircase under low light, and this picture is included. Later, when most of us were ready for bed, Emily decided to take pictures of her and her mother's room. Emily panned around the room, snapping off pictures, and caught one of the most daring pictures yet seen there at the Cashtown Inn—in the mirror of the bedroom dresser is seen in ectoplasm a 'cheesecloth' form of a woman. You can see a face of a woman if you look close up. You can see the couch and the wall through the female spirit in this mirror.

Exterior of the Cashtown Inn, Cashtown, Pennsylvania. Note that there are two hovering ectoplasmic 'mists' close to the front door, while 'others' appear out of windows above. Photo by Emily Grace Freed.

Emily Grace Freed's picture of a hovering brown ghost
on the Cashtown Inn lobby stairway.

The Cashtown Inn 'ghost woman' as seen in the dresser mirror in the Heth Room where Barbara Roberts and her daughter stayed overnight. Photo by Emily Grace Freed.

Close-up of the face of the 'ghost woman' caught by Emily Grace Freed

Reluctantly, I became the first to go up the lobby staircase, not knowing what to expect. I went up about five or six steps, and felt a military-uniformed force in front of me, then through me, making me very nauseated. I turned around to see Steve, Adele, Allen, and Jim Zero watching me near the landing as I stated emphatically, "There's a soldier standing right where I am—I think he is waiting for us." Both Steve and Allen got busy setting up their cameras to look up the staircase. Being lightheaded, I moved on up to the landing; the soldier was still there. I didn't get a negative feeling from the soldier, rather, more curiosity than anything. I could see the uniform in my mind; it was definitely Civil War period, namely from the South.

I moved up to the second floor. I could feel many soldiers now that we spent time in this building. Jim Zero and I moved into one of the rooms, and being shy, Jim asked me my impressions. I became very much aware that a soldier named (later learned was 'General') John Imboden spent time in one of the bedrooms upstairs, and could feel what I expected were messengers and liaisons coming and going. I was given a lower bowel impression, of which I remarked to Jim, "I think that John Imboden had some problem in his bowels or his prostrate." Jim later told me that this was true. General Lee moved the Confederate Army north into Pennsylvania, marched south through Cashtown searching for food, a small residential town perhaps best known for its orchards and farms, and later into Gettysburg. After my sister and I spent time upstairs, Adele and I expended more time in the lobby with some of the other ghost-hunters, wherein she heard the name "James P.," and could describe him walking his horse. Jim Zero excitedly remarked that Adele picked up on Brigadier General James Pettigrew, who was well-known for walking his horse amongst the soldiers, and who was involved in 'Pickett's Charge' on day three of the Gettysburg battle.

We spent some time in the basement level of the Cashtown Inn. I can tell you, I don't want to go back there again! I was nauseated the whole time down there; I could visualize in my mind arms and legs lying in a heap on one side of the basement, and see men sawing off limbs in another side. I was sick to my stomach. I did not stay long! It was strange, however, to see a stream of water running through an area of the basement. The owners as a general rule do not let visitors down there because of the problem with having water run through there, yet, there is some food storage that works nicely there as it remains cool even in the summertime. Allen Gross, our Spirit photographer, was able to get very good EVPs—electronic voice phenomena—throughout the house, including the basement. He also caught on video the spirit of a soldier hovering on the lobby stairs, right where I stated a soldier stood. I have included here some of the video photo stills with permission from Allen Gross to print here in the book. You can see a small bright white orb move up the stairs, go behind the banister at the top of the landing, dance somewhat on the top stairs close to the landing, and finally move off into the small dining/barroom. You can catch the short video of this on our website, which is stated at the back of this book.

I wish to mention here that I met Allen Gross in September 2006 after my friend/ client Lorraine F., suggested that I meet him. I drove up to Gettysburg to the Farnsworth Hotel on Baltimore Street and met Allen and his wife Vivian over dinner. Both of them are from the Roanoke, Virginia area. A likeable couple with deep Southern drawls, both know how to put one at ease, and to quick laughter. Allen stated that his interest in orb photography started a year earlier after he recovered from heart surgery. He felt drawn to Gettysburg, noticing that he got many different spirit emanations such as the orbs and ectoplasm showing up on film. Allen told me recently he now has over 200,000 such orb photos; many of them are now developing faces in the middle of the orbs. He hopes to come out with a book on orbs soon. I have included Allen Gross' address and contact number at the back of the book in case anyone wishes him to lecture or take pictures for groups.

An ectoplasmic horse and rider. Photo taken by Allen Gross.

I also want to state here that if the reader wishes to try to take pictures of orbs, it works best with a digital camera, as you can see your image right away. The image formed by the 'charged-coupler device' inside the camera is as sensitive to 'near-infrared' light as to visible light, so you can take pictures at night with the flash and have orbs appear. While some cameras with emulsion film may pick up orbs, you will not be able to see your picture until you have the film developed. The digital camera is superior to picking up orbs because of its low infrared frequency. The orbs' fluorescence (frequency) is triggered by use of the flash on the digital camera, and is aided by an abundance of free electrons and moisture in the atmosphere. The orbs therefore must be electromagnetic in nature. If you want to study orbs or spirit emanations more, get the book entitled, *The Orb Project*, by Miceal Ledwith, D.D., LL.D., and Klaus Heinemann, Ph.D. This is a thorough book written by a theologian and a physicist who feel that their serious investigation into orbs indicates "proof on the physical level that these orbs are not just 'frequencies' but realms of existence as real as our physical reality is to us. It must be asked that if these orb entities are not beings of this physical universe we inhabit, is it not possible they exist in other realms above ours."

It has long been Adele's and my understanding that Spirit finds ways to try to correct our misunderstanding of 'heaven.' Sightings of saints such as Mother Mary in Fatima of Portugal, Medjugorje of Bosnia-Herzegovina, El-Zeitoun of Egypt, and other apparitions through religious experiences as well as that of the Spiritualist movement from the Civil War period to the 1930's to today, work to give us an objective assessment of these phenomena regarding our place in these realms. Is it not possible that these orbs, these discarnate beings in our limited sense of perception, are allowing us to become aware of not only them, but perhaps of other sentient beings (dare might I say this?) such as those of unidentified flying objects and their inhabitants. Perhaps they dwell on a lower or finer dimension of existence here, right to the side of us as well! There are immense possibilities approaching all of us if we but open ourselves to these new realities. Isn't it possible that if these other realities exist, then there is a Divine architect after all?

In 1988 I, Allyson, went against the grain and worked in-house for one of my longstanding clients, Williams and Wilkins, Waverly Press in Baltimore, Maryland. As I was a graphic designer for what turned out to be my last year in this occupation, I was overworked in what turned into an impossible job. I managed to turn out 60 magazines, periodicals for one of the largest medical publishers in the world, yet, I needed more staff, and the bosses were unwilling. I managed to continue my metaphysical groups and readings, and felt unduly stressed during my marriage as well. So imagine how I felt when I started to see small lavender-blue 'bubbles' one evening when I answered the telephone when I was alone in the house! *Bloop, bloop, bloop*, they came, while I yakked on the telephone. I thought something was wrong with my eyes. Once they started, I saw them sometimes at night outside or in a darkened room; during the day, they would occasionally be seen at my office at Williams and Wilkins. I ventured to mention this to some of my friends and colleagues I trusted. An editor/writer friend of mine who also worked at the publishing company started having green orbs who visited. I wasn't sure *what* I was seeing then—I even spoke to a John Hopkins ophthalmologist about these 'bubbles.' Since I told him what I did 'on the side,' he concluded that nothing was wrong with my eyes. I felt relieved; however, some days at work the bubbles seemed to *want my attention.* One day, it came down to having so many of these bubbles, what I now know to be *orbs*, crowding my cubicle, vying for my notice, that I couldn't concentrate on what I was doing for the company. I remember mentally yelling at these orbs, "Look! You will all have to go away! I need to get some work done!" The orbs vanished hence. It has been years since I have seen orbs, but now and then I will see a bluish-purple orb in my house. It wasn't until I picked up *The Orb Project* book that the memory of the lavender-blue orbs came back. It won't surprise me that other people have had this same experience in their lives. Spirit emanations have been trying to get our attention for centuries.

Pauline Solomon inspecting her daughter Barbara Robert's new home
under construction. Note that most of what appears is dust,
but there are a few that are real orbs.

Fast-moving, peculiar orbs in front of a house. Photo by Barbara Menenghini.

Allyson—An Indian Named "White Ghost"

Late in 2005 I was at the New Visions Bookstore reading for individuals in an open platform group. I recall a cheerful woman in her forties hobbling in on what appeared to be metal crutches. When I came to her in the group, I asked for her first name and birth date—'Mary Jane' is her name, so we proceeded with the message. Nothing was out of the ordinary, until I told her that she had an American Indian standing behind her, wanting to introduce himself to her.

"Mary Jane, you have an Indian named 'White Ghost' who protects you. He has been with you for years and years, and I think he works not just with you, but with your family." I exclaimed. Mary Jane turned pale as a ghost, but didn't, or couldn't say anything right away. I moved on to start talking to the last person in the group, still glancing back at Mary Jane to see if she was recovering from her message. As I was winding up the messages and asking if there were comments or questions, Mary Jane spoke up.

"Allyson, I have to tell the group about White Ghost. When I was a little girl, my parents adopted me. My father later told me that I was one of twins born, but my sister died at birth. Dad was part Indian himself, and would sit out in the woods under a tree, appearing to talk to himself. When I was five years old, I remember joining him under the tree, and Dad would tell me he was talking to his spirit guide named White Ghost. Now it looks like White Ghost is working with me!"

The room was very still, but I was excited for Mary Jane, as this confirmed for the group that if I delivered this true message, then obviously, all the others were true. Little did I know that I was to see her about four months later at the same store with about five people in tow.

When this group finished, Mary Jane and her folks surrounded me to show me some pictures that Mary Jane took earlier in the week. "Allyson," she exclaimed," they must have known that I was going to see you again! Look at these pictures, and here is the story." Mary Jane handed me paper copies of two photographs, angled differently for me to see.

"I want you to know that when I went to bed on Sunday night, there was nothing on this living room table. When I woke up, got out of bed to put on coffee, I walked past the table to find the framed picture of Cochise that my father had given me. How it got to the table from the top of the mantle, I don't know! My Dad's green and white Indian beaded necklace surrounds the picture of Cochise; the necklace was in a drawer! Do you see the two little Indian dolls? My Dad gave me only one of them—where did the other doll come from?"

Hearing this, chills ran up my spine. I asked Mary Jane, "What about the rest of this? It looks like a box of bullets, a piggy bank, a red kitchen mitt, a tape dispenser and gun-cleaning powder. What do you make of that?"

Mary Jane shrugged, then said, "I think that White Ghost must have done all of this, to get my attention. My husband was still in bed when I saw this, so my first thought was to grab the camera and click away. I then went into the bedroom to see if my husband knew anything about what was on the table; he knew nothing about it. Do you think that this was White Ghost or Cochise?"

"I believe this was White Ghost, but I also think that it could also be your Dad and twin sister letting you know that they are with you from the spirit world. White Ghost is using the picture of Cochise to show you he is getting your attention, and yes, where did that second doll come from? It looks like it was apported to you, so that you have a doll from your twin sister. It may disappear eventually, it may not. What a wonderful gift!" I exclaimed.

I have included the pictures of the "White Ghost table" in the book to you to peruse. A wonderful example of apportation and the moving of objects from loved ones and spirit guides, all to help and assist Mary Jane in her spiritual evolution.

Two angles of the green and white Indian necklace framing a picture of Cochise. A pony blanket, two Indian dolls, a bullet box with a brass bear with a fish in its mouth were found by Mary Jane Glagola on her living room table.

Allyson—Mother Meera, the Avatar

Platform message groups became the staple of my profession during the eighties and nineties, especially in local bookstores. It not only allowed me to hone my psychic/mediumship abilities, it gave me a larger forum within to work. Unfortunately, the economics that allowed for the proliferation of bookstores changed by the late nineties—the larger "superstore" bookstores such as Barnes and Noble and Borders drove small New Age stores out of existence. The one store we aligned with metaphysics in Annapolis was also in danger, and I proffered my services there to help keep the shop in business.

I was involved one such evening in performing my duties there as a message-bearer. Twelve people came, hoping to hear from a loved one in spirit, and this the spirits accommodated as I worked through ten of the messages. The eleventh message, however, proved to be so extraordinary, that I include this anecdotal incident as another marker, or pillar of measurement in of evolution in this work.

I asked the eleventh person her first name, and her birth date. Adele and I want only the first name, as we do not want people to think that by having their full name would we have the capability to research them in any way. By having the client state just the name and birth date, we have enough 'voiceprint' to start hearing or seeing someone in spirit relay messages for the querying individual. This night, however, was truly unusual—that which came through was not a spirit or a ghost, but a bilocated, living human being!

Angie offered her name and birth date, and in my usual manner I started to deliver a message to her. As I did so, a golden, elongated cloud of energy appeared in my right peripheral vision. Out of this sparkling cloud stepped a tiny East Indian woman with a large red bindi, a circular mark between her eyes on her forehead. She ventured right over to my right side and stood there as I spoke to Angie—the top of her head came right up to my chin, she couldn't have been more than five feet tall. When I tried to look with full-frontal vision right at her, she disappeared, and when I went back to looking at the audience, then, again, the Indian woman was there. It made no sense to me what I was seeing, and the audience noticed my puzzled facial expression. One of the emboldened audience participants asked, "What's the matter? Is something wrong?" I looked around to the right again, and asked my audience, "Do you see this? Do you see the East Indian woman standing here?" Everyone shook their head no, and looked one at the other for their reaction. Shocked, I realized no one else saw the woman with her gold cloud, so I proceeded to tell the curious audience what transpired. Angie's face turned white, her eyes were as big as saucers. "I think I know who this is—do you get a name?" she asked. I hesitated a moment, listening. In the flash of a moment I heard, "Tell her 'Mother' is here. Tell her that she will be coming to see me. I am from India, but I do not live there now, I am in another country. She must come see me."

The Indian woman's voice came through strong and clear as a bell. In fact, it is rare to hear full, complete sentences from spirit, but this obviously was not spirit! Repeating the message to Angie (and the audience) caused an emotional reaction from Angie—her voice choked with emotion as she asked, "I know who this is, but I don't have the money to travel overseas right now! How am I to get to Germany?" A good question! I listened intently. A pause, then the Indian woman matter-of-factly stated, "Tell her not to worry about that. She is coming to Germany." With this, the petite dark-skinned woman got back into the golden chariot that was her cloud, and it dissipated like steam!

The platform group ended shortly thereafter; however, I felt like I was enveloped in an emotion of euphoric fog. All of my senses were drawn away from that room; all I could feel was 'palpable love and peace' (Georg Feuerstein stated this succinctly in his article, "The Mother," published in *Traditional Yoga Studies*). Angie, the lady who received the message from Mother Meera, would not leave the bookstore when I needed to close for the evening. I recall that she held onto my right arm tightly after the session so that I could not break to leave. She implored me to understand that if I could see Mother Meera, then the message was not just for her; it was also meant that Mother Meera was working with me as well. I vaguely remember her telling me this; all I wanted to do was go home. I finally pulled away, and with Angie in tow, we headed to our respective homes—mine was an hour away in Baltimore County at Gramercy Koinonia. For some unknown reason, I was truly tired after that session, when the norm for me is to be wound up like a top after working with the spirits. I fully expected this to be the end of my Mother Meera experience.

Two weeks passed. I would occasionally flash back to that evening in the Annapolis bookstore, and reminisce about the Indian woman with the gold cloud. Did this really happen? I thought so, but the skeptical part of me thought that this was a waking lucid dream. I tried to put this behind me.

Several more days passed. I just came home from working in York, Pennsylvania, and upon entering my apartment I called in for my phone messages, and Angie left one. Thank heaven I held the phone receiver away from my ear—Angie was fairly screaming with joy as she relayed her message concerning Mother Meera. Angie apparently told a close friend she knew the message that she received at the bookstore; now, mysteriously, money in lira, francs, and marks stuffed in envelopes addressed to her were showing up at her address. People from all over Europe were sending her money so she could come to Germany for darshan, a bestowal of grace and light through Mother Meera's gaze and touch.

I was amazed. Just simply astounded at this wonderful news.

Managing to find my voice, I graciously congratulated her on her good fortune, and after a few more words, I hung up. I know that I walked around in my head for the rest of that day. It wasn't too long thereafter that I was driving down Greenspring Valley Road near my home, that I had my second appearance of Mother Meera. I was driving to the bank located at Brooklandville Greenspring Station to make a deposit of checks. The face of Mother Meera floated just outside the windshield as I drove along pastoral fences, and just like that, she was gone. It was too vivid! Ten minutes later I was home, and called Angie Austin, hoping that she was home. Angie answered.

"Alright, Angie, what is happening? Mother Meera appeared in front of my windshield as I was driving near my home," I cried. "You tried to tell me several weeks ago that the Mother is working with me, too. But I don't understand this, I don't know her!" Truthfully, I had never heard of this woman whom Angie now was telling me was an *Avatar* of the Mother (the Shakti or the Holy Spirit) incarnated on the planet today. Where I had not been receptive to the idea in the Annapolis bookstore, Angie now had my full attention. "What exactly is an avatar?" I asked. Angie gently said, "An avatar is a great mystical being whose consciousness is Divinity, but is endowed with a human body. They are not simply human beings, or super—advanced mystics that have attained unity with the Divine through spiritual devotion and discipline, but rather they are beings that have descended to the earth plane, having taken on an earthly human form to aid the spiritual development of humankind. In this case, Mother Meera embodies the maternal aspect of the Divine Force."

"The Divine Mother has always been worshipped as the sustaining soul and force of the universe. Although some of the faces she wears are well known—Kali, the Virgin

Mary, Isis, for example—many of her embodied forms have chosen to work quietly in the world. In turbulent times such as these, several incarnations of the Divine Mother move among us, each with her particular task of healing or protection, or transformation."

I asked Angie if she knew any personal information about Mother Meera. "Yes, I do. Mother Meera was born on December 26, 1960 in the village of Chandepalle, in Andhra Pradesh, South India. If you go and look at the given birth dates of important figures in history, many of them are born within the last 12 days of the calendar year." I had to think about that. "Well, I don't believe that Jesus was born December 25th. A surprising number of the gods of the ancient classical world shared nativity stories that would later influence the development of the story of the birth of Jesus. Among those recorded are Tummuz of Mesopotamia, Attis of Asia Minor, Apollo and Dionysis of Greece, Mithras of Rome, and Baal of Palestine. The end of the calendar year has always been a time of celebration as the return of the sun, or the birth of the Midwinter King. Many celebrated in various ways, most often with fire—a symbol of hope—and with evergreen boughs that symbolize the circle of creation eternally. The Winter Solstice was the turning point of the course of the sun—the demise of the old and the birth of the new beginning. The reason I know this is because I have researching this data for a book I hope to write about St. Brighid." I continued. "The earliest date of a sign of celebration of the nativity of Jesus can be traced to 336 A.D., in Rome. It is possible that Jesus' birthday was celebrated January 6th—the present Twelfth Night—in line with the Eastern Orthodox Church. This is noted in a document known as the Philocalian Calendar, which dates from 354 A.D., but contains information contained in an earlier, lost document dating from 336 A.D. The early Christian Romans decided it was better to replace the festival of Saturnalia with the Christmas celebration." Angie broke in. "Yes, this is all true. Mother Meera chose to be born in December at this holiest of time. Her parents were farmers. She soon showed herself to be an unusual child—she would report 'going to various lights.' Her parents treated her as an exceptional child. They loved her very much, but they soon realized that Mother Meera needed more than they could provide. At the age of eight, Kamala Reddy (Mother Meera's birth name) was sent to live in the family home of her uncle Balgur Venkat Reddy. Mr. Reddy, himself, was living at that time in Pondicherry, at the ashram of Sri Aurobindo and Sweet Mother. Mr. Reddy prayed continually for the Divine Mother to come to him, and years passed with him waiting for a response. He returned home in 1972. He was convinced that the Divine Mother was living with him, when one day he was reading the newspaper one morning after Kamala was sent to school, despite her protestations that 'she didn't need school.' Mr. Reddy became disturbed by the sight of Kamala standing in front of him, and when he asked her why she wasn't in school at that hour, she calmly replied, "But Uncle, I *am* in school." With that reply, her image disappeared! Amazed and gladdened, Mr. Reddy prostrated himself, shouting for joy that the Divine Mother was now in residence in his very own home. From then on, Mr. Reddy became the confidant and protector of Mother Meera, and you can believe that she didn't go back to school long after that!" Angie laughed. "Mother Meera's work is to amplify the Light of the Divine on this planet, while ours is to open to this light completely. She encourages people to 'pray to the Supreme directly,' without any intermediaries, or else to pray through any 'incarnation' with whom one feels the greatest spiritual affinity. All are one."

I soon went and bought the book about Mother Meera entitled *The Mother by Adilakshmi: A Testament of Devotion*. I devoured this book, and then bought *Answers*, in which Mother Meera answers questions devotees have put to her over many years concerning her identity, her cause and work. Thalheim, Germany, is where she and her uncle, Mr. Reddy, settled after they traveled throughout Europe and Canada. On a third trip to Canada, Mr. Reddy's health deteriorated, necessitating a need for kidney dialysis, so they returned to Germany in 1981 for him and to see devotees. He urged her to buy a house in Thalheim in 1983, and she has continued to live there since his death in 1985. Mother Meera gives darshan in her new 'public home,' a former carriage and guesthouse that looks like a small castle, situated ten kilometers south-west of the medieval city of Limburg, just below Schloss Schaumberg.

I was now so fascinated by this little Indian avatar, I wanted to see her in Germany to receive her *darshan*, her gift of grace. I called Angie again to ask her when she was going. "I am going with Chet and Kallista S. on pilgrimage in June, do you want to come?" she asked excitedly. "I will send you the information about the tour, but you have to get your deposit in quickly. By the way, Chet and Kallista are coming to Washington, D.C. to give a talk. I think I will see if they will come and meet you."

They did in fact come along with Angie to visit—it seems that they were curious to meet the woman who had Mother Meera call in a most unusual fashion! During their visit, Chet mentioned that he had been to receive darshan many times at Mother Meera's home, and spent some of his time with other devotees in France. At the Mother's home in Thalheim, he is one of the rare people that ever received a vocal message from Mother Meera, as she normally does not speak during darshan. Once Chet pranamed, or bowed down to Mother Meera, she held his head in her delicate hands, a method she describes as 'undoing knots and obstacles in the individual's subtle body.' She gazed into Chet's eyes, calmly stating, "You are to marry." Her voice presumably startled many in the audience; this was not her usual way! Chet recalled that he answered her, exclaiming "Oh no, he was not to wed, besides, he was beyond the age to do so." Mother Meera gave her subtle dismissal, but this was not to be end of it! It was at a French home where a group of devotees were meditating, that Chet experienced Mother Meera appearing in a cloud. She pointed her right index finger at him, with a peculiar stare of her large round eyes, and pointed with her other hand to a young French woman in the room, who was unaware that the Divine Mother was there. Chet knew that the Mother was signaling him to understand that this selected woman was destined to be his bride and wife—Mother Meera chose Kallista.

Chet also explained that he was an author, and when he told me which book he wrote, I looked at him with surprise, got up and went to my bookshelf and pulled it down. "I have a story to tell you, Chet. I bought your book five years ago, and when I was halfway reading the book, I heard a voice tell me, 'One day you will meet the author.' I thought, 'Oh yeah, right!'" Not believing that it would ever occur, I laughed. Handing a pen to Chet, I asked, "Would you care to sign it?"

Chet did autograph his book, and my friend Stacey and I went on pilgrimage that summer. We very much enjoyed the darshan experiences at Mother Meera's house in Thalheim. During that week we visited an ancient Teutonic sacred mount, as well as the Cologne and Limburg Gothic cathedrals. A visit was made to the monastery of the medieval mystic healer and prophetess, Hildegarde von Bingen.

Stacey and I managed to go back later to see Mother Meera for darshan in two more trips. We stayed two out of three of those visits in Elz-Malmeneich at Zum Bergisches Land, or 'Patrick's Place,' as we called it, as we got to know the son of the owner rather well. Patrick was instrumental in showing us "Mary's Spring," the healing spring set back several miles into a deep forest, where the testimony of hundreds of crutches, canes, and other devices were left, because of miraculous healings claimed from drinking the water. We brought water back from Mary's Spring the last two times we traveled to Germany.

While staying at Zum Bergisches Land, we met many interesting folks from as far away as Canada, Belgium, and the United States. A gentleman named Elmer from Iowa was the fourth person to tell me to visit a Vedic astrologer in Washington, D.C., which I was to shortly follow-up to do—I always believe that heavenly messengers come in all forms! Stacey and I listened to numerous fascinating testimonials they wished to share concerning their observations of the Mother at work and play—as an artist, cook, seamstress, architect, construction worker, and gardener. We met a Belgian photographer who showed us pictures that he tried to take of the Mother when she worked in her Thalheim garden. Several photos showed nothing but a brilliant gold-white haze in the middle of the garden; other photos were normal, after he asked her permission for the opportunity to capture her likeness on film.

Our last trip to see Mother Meera was very special for Stacey and me. We opted to go see Mother Meera at her birthday—December 26—and this meant that we left Dulles Airport in Virginia on Christmas Day. We had some glitches in the trip going to Germany. Stacey had a Maryland artist work Mother Meera's portrait in pastels, of which Stacey and I have copies of the original. Limitations in size and weight of packages and luggage made it hugely difficult to get the crated painting past airport customs—we almost didn't get it into Germany for Mother Meera's birthday. Stacey used all of her cunning and persuasive verbal skills to convince the German airport authorities to let her keep it, crediting her work as a saleswoman! Once settled in the hostel (we couldn't get rooms at Patrick's Place), we soon found out that there were no restaurants open to foreigners that we could find, and the hostel served no food. Stacey had a hypoglycemic or low-blood sugar condition after flying for hours. We drove for miles in our rented Audi, looking in all the little villages for a place to eat. Exasperated, I finally stopped at a beer pub, threw open the doors, and bellowed out, "Does anyone here speak English? I need to know where I can find a restaurant!" I pantomimed in a preposterous, exaggerated makeshift sign language when it became clear that every blank, confused face in the barroom was obviously German. I heard a deep, male voice in the background yell back, "Yes, I know where you can go eat!" He was American! I followed the sound of the voice, heartened after driving for two hours and perhaps 60 miles looking for food, any food! The voice led me right up to the bar looking at a good-looking blonde, blue-eyed American bartender! I laughed out loud. "This is the last place I could think of, to get information for a restaurant!" And it was. He introduced himself as 'George,' and I explained to him that we did not eat on the airplane. But soon we were shown directions to the next village, and told to wait until 9PM for reservations, as he made a call to the local restaurant, helping out fellow peripatetic travelers!

The next night we eagerly anticipated taking the pastel painting with us to Mother Meera's home in Thalheim, just before darshan. (This was to be the last time we would have darshan at Mother Meera's home in Thalheim, as she moved it the following year to Limburg). Stacey hoped to be able to give it directly to Mother Meera. I didn't believe that would happen, and it turned out to be correct. Mother Meera's husband picked up the painting and delivered it to her room himself; he recognized us from other trips there. Stacey may have been disappointed, but we both had a marvelous time at that night's darshan, for we were both allowed to sit within proximity of Mother Meera that evening, the closest we were ever to view the Mother.

Perhaps it was because it was this little Indian avatar's birthday that we experienced the most interesting night of all. While she transforms others by the medium of silence, we could not help but notice the physical phenomena that occurred after twilight. She appeared to be surrounded by gold and colored lights that shone while she performed her work of imparting peace, healing and bliss. No pujas or outer adulation is performed. While waiting to receive darshan, we enjoyed watching, praying, and relaxing in our chairs. Moments brought new revelations. We simultaneously experienced smelling roses and other fragrances as it enveloped us—we were certain that the lights and the smells were 'visitors' from other spheres. When it came time to approach her and have her place her hands on my head, I felt my heart banging against my ribcage, and I shook from excitement as she looked me in the eyes. Ernest and heartfelt, I earlier prayed that the Mother would allow me one small boon—I wanted to see her Universe! I found myself staring, and the next thing I knew, I was pulled into the polestar which is her left eye, and that was the last thing I experienced that evening in the room! Part of me zoomed out into the solar system and beyond. I vaguely felt myself in my physical body as Stacey piled me into the car to head over to Patrick's Place for a late light dinner after darshan. My bliss had me soaring through novas, past millions of nebulas, sparkling stars and gas planets in black velvet space! The restaurant at Zum Bergisches Land, with Europeans and Americans relating their darshan experiences that evening over food and drink, was what brought me back to earth, but my 'flight' lasted nearly an hour! Stacey understandably knew that I was having an out-of-body experience, and propped me up while many of us were swapping stories of Mother Meera, and other spiritual journeys. Like a dreamer awakening, I eventually joined in the banter by relating some of my earlier experiences of Paramahansa Yogananda. The evening moved too swiftly; the little hotel restaurant pushed us out, as they wanted to close up. About eight of us edged closer to our rooms; roommates and new friends were hesitant to turn in for the night. Being tired from our airline trip, Stacey and I eventually trooped up the stairs to our room. As we headed down the corridor in front of our room, we both suddenly noticed the overpowering aroma of sandalwood which permeated for about four feet square around! We shouted for others in our restaurant group to come experience the sandalwood fragrance; all agreed that this was a wonder. The scent of sandalwood lingered for about thirty minutes right in front of the room. The little French woman who had the room across from ours raced into her hotel room, thinking that a perfume bottle must have broken. Stacey checked our room as well, but there were no fragrances to be smelled inside either room. I whispered, "It's Yogananda, Stacey, I know it! Who else exhibits the scent of sandalwood? I tell you, it's Paramahansa Yogananda! We were just talking about him downstairs—I know he dropped by here for a visit with dear Mother Meera, God be praised!"

Memories of that night in Germany will stay with me forever. Now when I gaze at the starry heavens, I think of Mother Meera and her large, soulful eyes. Her portrait hangs alongside Paramahansa Yogananda's portrait in my bedroom, where I meditate and send devotion daily.

Allyson—Visions, Astral Travel and Levitation

While I was still a little girl, waking visions would visit, creating startling moments. Most people do not ever receive such clairvoyance, which if you recall, is another way to describe what psychics call 'clear vision.' This type of clairvoyance, however, differs from the general type of 'second sight'—most psychics would generally state that this kind of clairvoyance they perceive is seen in the 'mind's eye.' That is, they see these things called visions in their head, while aware of their surroundings. Waking visions are different! They occur by forcibly arresting your normal field of vision, such as your day-to-day environment, and replace it with something else! There is no reason why a waking vision occurs without warning. It just happens.

The first waking vision came forth when I was about ten years old. I recall that I was in my bedroom alone, putting on my pajamas just before retiring. The room was dark, but the bedroom door was ajar, letting the hall light filter in across the bedroom floor. Just as I managed to get both arms and head pulled through the pajama top, I heard a popping sound in the room. I looked to the left, and all that was in the room disappeared, save for myself. I beheld what appeared to be the map of the United States and Canada in front of me, as though I was floating far, far above it. I recall seeing the northern states delineated, as well as the Canadian provinces. I remember seeing 'British Columbia' and 'Alberta' provinces spelled out, as well as 'Nova Scotia' and 'Prince Edward Island.' I heard a deep, male voice speak, "Someday you will be there." I had an inner knowledge, too, that in one or two of those places, I might spend days, if not months of time in Canada. To date, there has been a voyage to Nova Scotia in 1981; I was involved in returning a forty-foot Long Islander boat back to Annapolis, Maryland. The boat belonged to two National Geographic members, one of whom had Alexander Graham Bell as a great-grandfather. Bell's summer home is in Baddeck, Nova Scotia—Washington D.C. was too hot for his experimentations in summer.

The second major vision I had warned me of the impending car accident I was to endure. This was the only waking vision that had a purposeful logic! As I grew in stature and in knowledge, the visions became more frequent, but not necessarily with a map to explain their purpose.

The next waking vision had no reason to transpire, and who is to know why it occurred? I was living with my first husband in Edgewater, Maryland at our farmhouse by the water. I was cleaning our bedroom with the vacuum when I dropped the vacuum wand. I bent over to pick it up when I heard a popping sound, the kind where a champagne bottle is uncorked. I looked to find the location of the sound. The bedroom disappeared, and all I could see in front of my face is a garden, with colors more vivid than real life. Flowers, grass, and trees moved violently in their vibration. I looked left to right—it all moved with a sound, similar to a humming sound. I know that sound now—it vibrated to OOMMMM. The image of the garden lasted seconds, but the vision has stayed with me for a lifetime.

Why would Spirit show me a garden? I had a garden that I tended when I lived in Edgewater. I like to think that one of my guides wanted me to see a little garden in Heaven! Given the *when* and *where* of the vision, it didn't make sense. It might have to wait until another clue comes along to piece the puzzle together.

There are other visions that have come forth, and they are tied to the future. If there is a certainty about the future, some events must play out before other incidents come into being. I think that most visions give us a roadmap of the future.

Astral travel has only occurred twice in my life, and again, I had no control when it happened. I was still living in Edgewater when the astral traveling began. My first husband, Bernie, and I spent vacations bare-boating in the British Tortolas. We brought another couple with us to split the cost of the boat for a week, bringing food, drink, and other necessities onboard. The marina where we rented the boat had such beautiful plants and flowers that I wished that there was a way to transplant them to Maryland. There might have been a way for them to live indoors, if I could have supplied the necessary humidity and heat for them to survive. The vivid colors of croton—green, red, yellow, and orange—so beautiful! I suppose that my will kept it alive there, deep in my unconscious mind.

Bernie accepted a dinner invitation with friends from Washington, D.C. We drove in to the District, where my husband met with four of his school friends from University of Maryland. Bernie had a great time, but virtually ignored me. Not one of his friends or their wives seemed interested in me, I think, because there was a seven-to-ten year difference in our ages. I was forced to sink into my inner self for lack of attention. I recall my daydream about the British Tortola marina. Dreaming about standing at the water's edge, looking at the pier with four of the bareboats tied up. Parrots squawked. I could feel the wind blowing, the fine white sand between my toes, hear the rustling of the croton bushes nearby. The scene was paradise! I looked out over the bay, and felt water lapping up against my feet. It startled me to feel the water. Looking down at the water, my breath exhaled suddenly . . . I jerked back to the table with a crash of my cup on the floor! I nearly fell out of my chair, with everyone laughing at me. Bernie thought I fell asleep, and spoke of it derisively. I said nothing, but begged pardon for breaking the cup. I know that I was back at that marina. The water did lap at my feet!

Paramahansa Yogananda wrote of the ability of his guru, Sri Yukteswar to bilocate. Sri Yukteswar, a modern Yogi-Christ, was able to astral travel to the boardinghouse where Paramahansa Yogananda was living while in college, to warn him that his arrival by train was delayed. Yogananda experienced not just an apparition of Sri Yukteswar, but a fully materialized flesh-and-blood form! Apparently, Sri Yukteswar could be seen in two places at once.

When someone develops the ability to astral travel, the astral body is able to disconnect from the physical form by means of an 'astral cord connection' to travel wherever it wishes. If this is possible, then the mind, as we know it, transcends the physical body, and is in fact housed in the larger and finer essences that are called bodies connected to the physical. The fact that scientists are now reaching the conclusion that human beings use only ten percent of their brains may explain the ability to have waking visions, astral travel and levitation.

Levitation is the ability to defy the law of gravity. Is this only possible of special persons perceived to be saints or spiritual sages? I believe that levitation is possible with ordinary people who have learned to focus their God concentration intently. Paramahansa Yogananda wrote of a levitating saint, Bhadhuri Mahasaya of India, who was able to remain in the air. Sri Mahasaya expertly mastered the various pranayamas, or methods, of controlling the life force (prana) through regulation of breath. These pranayamas are mentioned in the eightfold yoga outlined by Patanjali, the foremost ancient exponent of yoga. Yogananda claimed that a yogi's body loses its grossness after perform certain pranayamas.

Levitating saints of the Christian world such as Sr. Joseph of Cupertino, Italy, (Giuseppe da Cupertino, 1603-1663), exhibited a worldly absentmindedness, where he was known as the 'Flying Saint.' His monastery brethren could not allow him to serve in a waiting position at the common tables, lest he ascend to the ceiling with the dishes. Often he was known to float in the atmosphere when he came upon a holy statue; St. Joseph and the stone statue would be seen levitating together. When he attended a papal audience at the Vatican, Joseph was so overwhelmed upon meeting Pope Urban VIII (pope from 1623-1644) that he rose into the air, and only descended when ordered so by a superior. Joseph's flights were unannounced and apparently uncontrollable for him, at least on a conscious level; he was often apologetic for his strange behavior, although it continued as an embarrassment for the Church.

St. Joseph of Cupertino, Italy, known as the 'Flying Saint.'

Physical elevation was disconcerting for St. Theresa of Avila (1515-1582). Known to hold many organizational responsibilities, she vainly tried to prevent her 'uplifting' aerial experiences. "But little precautions are unavailing," she wrote, "when the Lord will have it otherwise."

The physical phenomena medium D.D. Home of England was well known for levitation through windows and doors. Attested by Oliver Wendell Holmes, Elizabeth Barrett Browning, and many others interested in spiritualist principles in the nineteenth century, Home claimed that his spirit guides would perform these aerial feats for the purpose of opening closed minds. Worldly people do not care for the frankness that shatters worldly delusions. Obviously, another factor is at work to defy the law of gravitation. It is a union with the Universal Presence, of God. It is a choice made by the soul, exhibited in an outward manner through consciousness. The world's ado offers Masters nothing that God cannot provide.

I offer the reader two examples of levitation, which I experienced. The first illustration came when I was deep in my thoughts at Towsontown Centre in Baltimore in 1991. Known for my capacity to turn off extracurricular noise and distraction, I was busy walking through the mall after completing a purchase. I was determined to get back to my car in the parking lot, but found myself absorbed with thoughts that pertained to later in the day. When a child strayed in front of me, my eyes caught the child, and with a loud thud, I felt *both feet* hit the floor hard! I realized that after getting off the escalator, I "walked on air" for about ten paces when the distraction of the child brought me back to earth. I found it difficult now to resume my level of concentration, and clumsily managed to leave the building. Two months later, another incident occurred, but this time the levitation was documented and conveyed to me by another individual. Audrey Smallwood Lawson, a medium from Baltimore, witnessed such an occurrence at Camp Chesterfield in Indiana. She was not, however, forthcoming as a witness right away; Audrey only told me in confidence once she came to know me. Here is her story:

> "Allyson came to Camp Chesterfield with a friend of hers when I was there the week that members of my church attended. Several of the mediums living on the grounds insisted that two other visitors were there from the Baltimore area, that we should meet each other. I recall seeing Allyson and Katherine walking about the property, going to and fro from the hotel, cafeteria, museum, and classes. I saw them several days later in the common area near the small cemetery, and it was then that I saw both Allyson and Katherine *walking on air*, about two feet off the ground. My heart jumped out of my body as I hit my friend, saying, "You see that, you see that, look, look, *look!*" The hair on my neck rose—sometimes spirit will do these

things to get our attention. I admit that I was not always so comfortable with spirit physical phenomena, and this was certainly one of those moments!"

"Allyson learned who we were, and pursued trying to be friendly towards me. I was very cautious, in fact, I was fearful of someone who could levitate! I avoided her at all costs. She and Katherine ran into our group at a restaurant in Anderson, and of all of the restaurants there are there—about fifty—why did she end up here at the same place as us? I felt like spirit was making this happen, like spirit was 'closing in" on me, saying that there were 'no hiding places.' Allyson, on the other hand, was genuinely interested in meeting me, and when I learned that we lived not more than a mile away from each other in Baltimore, it was then I knew spirit made this levitation happen just for me."

Audrey Smallwood Lawson, Baltimore, Maryland

Lifting of the Veil: Physical Phenomena Mediumship

Early one August 2007 Saturday morning I wrenched open the door to New Visions Bookstore in York, Pennsylvania, to hear a spirit voice whisper "You are going to find *the book* here." As I often need a couple of coffees to get my ignition started so early in the morning, driving from Annapolis, Maryland, to make it on time to begin readings 97 miles away, I wondered if I wasn't imagining this. Striding into the bookshop, easily setting up my computer, I settled in for a day of readings in the morning, a short lunch, and an afternoon of mini-readings in the platform mediumship group. Many are newcomers to the mediumship circle, nervous as they walk in the door, but afterwards, many straggle to leave, so eager and happy for the messages from loved ones they receive. Finishing the platform message circle early today—an hour earlier than normal, left me enough time to find that book Spirit wished me to locate.

The hour passed. I wandered throughout the store, not certain exactly what I was to buy. I kept looking at the backside of a book facing outward on a book shelf, the photo of the author drawing me back several times. She, the author, was like a magnet, and I did not know why. The store owner quietly let me know he was getting ready to close. I went back to the book, turned it over, and with astonishment, laughed out loud. *Bridging Two Worlds*, authored by Dr. Marti Barham, is about the author, who, along with her mediumistic husband Jay, and a group of students, sat regularly for Spirit to demonstrate physical phenomena mediumship. I could not speak for several minutes. It was just the tool I was looking for in my own work.

A medium friend of mine, Hoyt Robinette, strongly suggested for three years that Adele and I start sitting for physical phenomena mediumship. Try as I might, the sittings were haphazard, life got in the way! I felt frustrated in my efforts to convince Adele that we must do this, but I knew it would help if we could interest others—clients or not—to sit with us. Several months leading up to this discovery of the book, I was receiving very strong messages from one of my spirit mentors, a woman by the name of Ethel Post Parrish Riley to start sitting.

Ethel in her own time had been an outstanding medium, internationally famous due to six infrared photographs taken of her sitting in the medium's cabinet for a materialization séance at the Temple of Truth Church at Camp Silver Bell in Ephrata, Pennsylvania. (You can go to *www.Survivalebooks.org-SBell.jpg.htm* to see the series of these pictures on the internet). Her Indian spirit guide, Silver Bell, is seen in these photographs as materializing from under the black cloth of the cabinet. In the sixth photograph, Silver Belle is as solid as you and I. I was told by Reverend Reed Brown of the Arlington Metaphysical Church in Arlington, Virginia, that Silver Bell was known to not only materialize, but could speak and was known to be 'warm to the touch' when she allowed people in the séance to touch her or her garments.

Ethel has been working with me since I first heard of her when I was "shanghai-ed" in 1990 by Helen G., a medium from Andrews Air Force Base (located close to Washington, D.C.), to Ephrata, Pennsylvania for an afternoon mental mediumship demonstration led by Reverend Virginia Falls. In the evening, a medium from another town was to demonstrate 'trumpet mediumship.' Helen was keen on participating in the trumpet demonstration—I didn't have any idea at that time what this was about. We drove to the Camp Silver Bell church that weekend, now Ethel's church after the Temple of Truth camp split, located in the basement of the motel on Route 222 between Lancaster and Ephrata. We signed up for the afternoon with Reverend Falls, but only Helen could get into the trumpet demonstration, as it was filled. Another demonstration was available the next day, Sunday, and I signed up for this group which featured 'card precipitation.' Little did I know that the best laid plans can go awry, but they did so in the most unusual way.

Helen was not happy when I told her I signed up for the card precipitation group on Sunday; she wanted to drive back that night after the trumpet demonstration. Someone in spirit whispered to me, "No, you will be staying overnight." A gruff, no-nonsense, dominating woman, Helen said adamantly, "We are not staying overnight, we are going home later." I kept quiet, knowing that events wouldn't turn out her way.

The demonstration led by Reverend Virginia Falls was rather uneventful—I cannot at this writing remember anything other than a general message given to me. What I do remember, however, was the wall facing the front door as you enter the church in the lower level of the motel. It was filled with images of many faces imprinted on silk. Some of the faces were in color, looked painted-on or photograph-like. Some of these faces were large, with others very tiny, some looking like lead-pencil smudges. One of these 'silk precipitations,' a piece of cloth about 8" x 12" had every inch covered with faces. I recall a 3" x 5" index card next to it, stating that the recipient of this silk precipitation knew every face on that silk. I was entranced, indeed mesmerized. There were many card precipitations there as well—names of loved ones, spirit guides, drawings, and messages. I could hardly tear myself away from this—I wanted to learn more.

We had dinner with several others who were waiting to participate in the trumpet séance, and one of the women I met was Gloria Cook. Even though I did not know much about astrology at that time, I swear now that Gloria had to be a Sagittarian sun, moon, or ascendant-born. She was the stereotypical bleached blonde in her 60s, with an avid interest in teaching metaphysical matters. Gloria had a car trunk full of crystals, jewelry, and knickknacks that she laid out in her motel room to sell; I bought a crystal pendant with matching earrings that I still own. That evening, Helen and others went their way to sit for the trumpet séance, while I wandered around the motel conversing with Gloria Cook. Soon afterwards, most of the crowd came back, sorely disappointed that the trumpet did not lift, with Helen complaining the loudest. It was my private observation that the trumpet would not lift with her in the room! More people started to come into Gloria's motel room, looking for something to do, when Helen suggested we have our own séance. Several men joined the party, but stated flatly they wanted to go find a restaurant; they did not stay. Soon we had the lights turned out with a prayer of protection given by a lady named Carol K. As soon as she sat down, the room went quiet, and I could see faint light coming through the drawn blinds. Letting my eyes adjust, I noticed several columns of hazy white light standing in a corner where the room was darkest. I grabbed Carol's wrist, and could not help myself when I gasped, "I see several columns of energy over there in the corner!" No one seemed to be impressed by my enthusiasm. Someone softly spoke, "Ask for names, see if you can hear names." I let my mind go blank, and I heard a name call out 'White Cloud.' I spoke the name out loud to the group. As I did so, the column of energy moved over to where Helen was sitting cross-legged on the bed. It overshadowed her, transfiguring a few inches in front of Helen into the most handsome of Indian men. White Cloud's energy could be seen as a transfigured man of about thirty years of age, with flowing black hair and a wonderful physique, sitting cross-legged as well. All of us present could see him. Several more mediums transfigured, and you can imagine I was transfixed. I felt strange, however. I felt extremely cold, almost numb, and very nauseated. Carol managed to shake my hand off hers, stating I was cutting off her circulation. Helen and the others spoke of seeing a man in biblical robes with a short beard standing right in front of me. Funny, I could not see this, and said so. Carol next to me told me, "You can't see it . . . you can't see it if it is happening in front of you or right next to you. You can see transfiguration only if it is happening to someone else in front of you or at an angle, but not next to you or on you." I thanked her for that piece of information, which I have gladly shared with other students in my time.

During our séance, a thunderstorm broke loose. Between lightning splits and roaring thunder, Gloria Cook spoke up, "My God, it looks like an angel is forming right above Allyson. Can everyone see this?" Upon hearing this, I was so cold that I felt like I was sitting inside of a glacier. I was so numb I could hardly turn my head. I didn't understand that Spirit was pulling energy out of my body to formulate spirit selves so that the other mediums present could see them. I heard in my head that the angel was my longtime angel friend, Ariel, and I said so to the group. Carol next to me, stated, "Well, if you are an angel, make something happen in the room." I turned my head as best I could to look at Carol, but my left arm automatically lifted across me and pointed at the heart area of Carol. Spirit spoke through me, asking, "Can you feel this, can you feel this?" Sarcastically, Carol shot back, "Can I feel WHAT?" The next thing I knew, a bolt of white energy, like lightning, came out of my arm and burst either in front of Carol or hit her in the chest region. All I recall is she fell back onto the bed that she and I shared—she was knocked unconscious. The bolt of energy affected me as well. It cut me loose from the trance state, and I fell back easier, but I stayed aware of what transpired. The oldest woman in our group, Jane, reached over, shouting frantically, "We've got to help her," but Helen grabbed the woman, exclaiming, "No, don't touch her, you can't do that! She will come around." Helen was right—Carol came to about five minutes later, with a less superior attitude from then onwards. The lights were back on in the motel room, and everyone wanted to recap what exactly happened, including me. Jane would not leave me alone; she was constantly asking me questions such as "where did you study mediumship, what organizations do you belong to?" Perplexed, I answered her questions with the truth that I did not have teachers or organizations that I belonged to up to that time, I had been going at this alone. Jane didn't believe it.

Helen and I found out during the séance that the thunderstorm was not about to let up to allow us to drive back to Maryland. As I was driving, I didn't trust the brakes on that boat of a car Helen owned. Helen reluctantly gave in and we spent the night at the motel. At seven o'clock in the morning, Jane was knocking on the door with more questions! Helen murmured to me from her twin bed, "Forget Jane. I'm not entertaining anyone this early in the morning." I silently agreed; neither of us answered the door. Jane would have to wait until we all got together for brunch at 11AM.

All of us came together at the aforementioned brunch, but Helen refused to stay for the card precipitation group. I pled for her to stay, but she was adamant, so we left for home. About a week later, Helen called me to tell me that Carol K. had a card that came through 'by proxy' for me. What this means is even though I had signed and paid for a seat in the card precipitation group but didn't show up, a card nevertheless was delivered for me, and in this case, it was from someone I did not expect to come through.

The card was drawn and signed by my long lost baby brother, Jeff. There was no one in the entire group that weekend who knew me well enough to know about my lost sibling.

On the left, the first card precipitation Allyson received in 1990 from her brother Jeff by proxy, medium unknown. Middle, a card precipitation received in 2004 through the mediumship of Gladis Stroehme. He added a faint halo, angled around his head. On the right, Jeff as he appears a little older, now working as one of the spirit physicians (chemists) with Allyson. Card received in 2007 through the mediumship of Hoyt Robinette.

Many years have passed, and now Adele's and my group began sitting in September 2007. We use my lower recreation room, closing off all windows, sliding glass door and hallway with heavy-duty black plastic. I came up with an idea of using wooden frames covered with plastic to easily shut out light for the windows. Another innovative frame was designed for the sliding glass door and hallway, which Andrew T., our resident carpenter in our group constructed for the group. This has made it very easy to cover all light-emitting agencies, allowing one person to set up within a half-hour. It has also reduced the need for blue masking tape.

Through many months of sitting our group was mainly women, with Andrew T. our one open-minded 'token' male. We have now seen how the group has become more balanced with three more men joining our collective.

Dr. Marti Barham was correct when she stated in her book, *Bridging Two Worlds*, that it takes great patience to sit when nothing happens for months. It took about two and a half months for noises such as tapping, rapping, banging, and clicking to start. We have had ectoplasm swirl around the middle of the circle, in many cases members of the group would feel someone touching their hair or hands. Cold sometimes envelopes us, causing hair to stand on end. There may be nothing for several more weeks. Then, when some members do not show for various reasons, it starts up again with vigor. We have added musical instruments such as a drum, rainstick, bells, castanets, and shakers, hoping that spirit would like to make music.

We have found that burning incense, sage, or sweetgrass before meeting helps in altering the atmosphere in the room. It either calms or rejuvenates many of the participants depending upon how their day commenced. We have tried singing Christmas carols and other songs, but not many in the group have 'singing voices.' We instead substituted light music in the background, and found this has helped enormously.

About three months into sitting, we had a castanet start 'clack-clack-clacking.' The night this happened, we were missing a mother and daughter from our group. We started to wonder if certain people may or may not help the group. Emily, the daughter, had just left a relationship, and was in chaos emotionally. I mentioned to Barbara, her mother, it might be better for Emily to not be there while she sorted out her life. I made it clear within the first two sessions that negative emotions such as anger and sadness prevent much spirit communication. I even suggested that if people are sick, it is better not to attend. We have kept to these rules steadfastly.

Curiously, visuals and sound may not be seen or heard by all in attendance. When the castanet began clacking, several individuals at the end of the room nearest to the sliding glass door heard it as it was, on the floor underneath the small table holding the bells and trumpets. Andrew, Adele, Marilyn, and I heard it as if it was being held up near the ceiling in the eastern side of the house. This gave us the realization that visuals and sound are perceived differently by those in the room.

The same week that we had the castanet make noise, I visited a male medium named Reverend Mike Perry, hoping to connect with some of the mediums I knew in spirit, to see if all is right with what we are doing. Mike did not know me until that day, and when my reading began, he mentioned, "There are a great number of mediums in the room with us. Several here say you know them. The first to step up is Ethel Post Parrish Riley. She mentors you. Another is Reverend Gladis Stroehme—she says to me, *Allyson is a mouthpiece*, you are a mouthpiece. You knew her, right?" As Mike was wearing a blindfold, I vocally answered, "Yes, I knew Gladis, but I only know Ethel from visiting her church in Ephrata, Pennsylvania, many years ago."

"There are more mediums here—physical phenomena mediums, Allyson. There is a Reverend Virginia Falls here. You met her once." Mike added. I exclaimed, "Yes, I did meet her once, and again, that was at the church in Ephrata."

"Well, there is Ethel Post Parrish Riley, Reverend Kathryn Kuhlmann, Reverend Virginia Falls, and also a Reverend Warren Smith here, too. He says you didn't know him personally, but he knows you because you talk about him." I laughed, saying this was true; I have told some stories I have heard from Reverend Reed Brown of the Arlington Metaphysical Church in Arlington, Virginia about Reverend Warren Smith. "It looks like you are sitting to develop physical phenomena, Allyson—that is what they are telling me." Mike mused. Although I only had a half-hour for a reading, I acknowledged to Mike that our group only started several months earlier, and I wished that we had longer to talk. He had to hold to a schedule, and I hope to see him again later.

Several weeks later, we had a strange physical phenomena occur. Even though we use a red light on a dimmer to help our eyes adjust to the darkness going in and coming out, once the red light is out, the room is so dark, *nothing* can be seen. There is not one iota of white light. Everything, including the oil radiators and boombox, has black tape to cover all light factors. We have since noticed that even though the room is so completely black, that all present have noticed the room get 'brighter,' as if the room is lit by moonlight, then go black again. This has happened several times in each sitting. We have also noticed strange 'light' around the trumpets. A strange 'glint.' Adele and I have seen a phosphorescent glow when sitting with Reverend Reed Brown. We have also seen the narrow ends of the trumpets appear hazy, wavering slightly. We have now added a piece of paper with tracings of the large ends of the trumpets on it, leaving the trumpets in place—to see if the trumpets will move. We shall yet see!

On Thursday, January 3, 2008, we had a visible white light flash on and off in an upwards pattern. Barbara, Lorraine, and myself, Allyson, were sitting on the eastern end of the room, when we all saw this. My twin sister was sitting in the makeshift cabinet we call 'the cave' (because it is an alcove underneath the stairs, designed at one time to fit a double bed). The cabinet has two black sheets velcroed to the opening. We all take turns sitting one at a time in the cabinet, and tonight was Adele's turn. We decided that this evening to add some music, by Chuck Wild, titled *Liquid Mind: Ambience Minimus*. It is so soothing, and has an OM sound quality that runs continuously through the CD, with no breaks. We all noted that we liked this, as our singing is not up to par!

Barbara mentioned out loud that she saw a red rectangular-shaped light to the left, perhaps on the wall. It moved slowly upwards, and as it did so, it turned red to a very bright white light. Barbara stated "I could see the color changing so that the tip turned white first and the white moved down the column of light until all the red changed to white. It stayed in sight for a few seconds, then it disappeared. As I watched the light, both Allyson and Lorraine saw the light and commented about it."

I was talking out loud to the group when I saw the light. A very bright white, tear-shaped light that moved upwards, yet, I saw it as though it was flashing on, then off, then on again. Both Barbara and Lorraine saw this. But it wasn't until the following day, that I had a flashback to what I saw—I realized that I saw the light flash *onto* what appeared to be *undulating folds of grayish cloth*. I could see cloth through the tear-shaped light, about a foot in width and length. I called Barbara and Lorraine that night to see if they themselves saw this, but they did not. I saw the earliest formation of an ectoplasmic human figure. It looked like clothing on someone in spirit. Emotionally, I was on a high. I wondered why everyone in the group could not see this? It turns out that four out of nine people saw the lights. Adele, who sat in the cabinet couldn't see it, obviously. It must be due to everyone's evolving consciousness.

Marilyn sat closest to where the flashing light appeared. I saw the light as though it was about two feet in front of her, but Marilyn fiddled with the oil radiator switches, thinking that they were causing us to see the bright white light. All four of us stated "no, that's not it!" Anyway, what you could see of the switches was a faint orange color, and as they are covered with black duct tape, I am not sure that it would affect anything manifesting in the room. Since this night, a triple layer of black tape has been applied to the radiator switches; no more light emanates into the room at all. We have since garnered more ghostlike shining forms appearing in our darkroom; we await these spirits desire to take on more solid physicality, hopefully to speak for themselves.

Several weeks later, this session began with six of us—Edie, Marilyn, Andrew, Allyson, Lorraine and me, Adele. After talking about several books to be given out to us for reading, Andrew sat down in the cabinet and closed the curtain. We were chatting about recent events in our lives as Allyson turned down the red light, first low, then completely off. After a few moments, Edie and Marilyn exclaimed that the room seemed extraordinarily dark. Several members commented about a soft white light emitting from behind Allyson's chair. She quickly turned around in her chair, thinking the red light was somehow still lit, but it was turned off. The light seemed to glow ever so brightly, then fade. All the while, we would talk about what we could see. I told the group I heard the name of 'Shooting Star,' followed not long after with the name of 'Crazy Horse.' Allyson announced to us that Barnabas was present with us; she allowed him to 'borrow' her to come in and talk to us.

About five minutes passed before Barnabas spoke through Allyson, with a thick, low accent. He greeted us with praise for continuing the circle, assuring us that phenomena would be forthcoming in the months ahead. He assured us that the highest of the spirit community were with us and were pleased with what we have been doing. Barnabas then interrupted his talk by remarking that 'Daisy,' Allyson's joy guide, had several spirits who wanted to come through, so he said his good byes and left.

Daisy made herself known by saying 'hi' to our group in her usual high-pitched voice. She said several people wanted to come in and announce themselves to our group. Shortly afterwards, a booming male voice fairly shouted out, "Tall Oak, Tall Oak!" We welcomed him, and he exhorted Andrew for staying with the circle. "You are like chieftain with many wives." Tall Oak paused, adding afterwards, "Maybe I should not say that!" Our group laughed at these remarks. He told Andrew that he was his protector, 'like a tree, he was his shade when he worked outside in nature.'

Three more American Indians came in through Allyson to speak to our ensemble. 'Black Kettle' announced his name; we greeted him, but after a brief interim, he said, "The person I came to talk to is not here for me." He spoke briefly, then he allowed 'Crazy Horse,' who had a hoarse, raspy voice, come in, calling out his name to us. I was surprised and yet delighted, as it confirmed the spirit voice in my head before Barnabas channeled through Allyson. Crazy Horse told us hat "he was here for the whole group. Many Indians have their bows and arrows drawn, forming a circle around us while we conduct the spirit circle." All of us exclaimed out loud, not realizing the extent of the protection we had from so many well-known brave warriors. Finally, Chief Red Cloud came in, saying his name in a low, soft voice. I was amazed at his coming for he is one my Indian protectors. "The other Indians are young, and I am ancient, you understand?" He asked the group if we knew the signs of nature. No one responded, so he said "read the clouds, and know nature. I will be with the sun as it sets to show red in the sky. The clouds will help you to understand nature." He also said the drum and the rattles would start making noises in the middle of the room, and the noise would be created by him. He then said, "Someone has an arrowhead in this group." I exclaimed yes, with surprise, that I had one. "Bring the arrowhead to the circle and place it with the other objects in the middle, it will help."

Red Cloud paused, as if he was listening to someone, and said that Daisy had others that wanted to come in. He said goodbye, and to everyone amazement, Allyson's best friend, Stacie, a young beautiful woman who died from cancer two years earlier came in, announcing her name. "You know who I am, my name is Stacey. I am "Ah-lee-san"s friend." I laughed at her way of pronouncing Allyson's name with an Oriental twang. When Stacie was alive, this was her way of teasing my sister. She called my name, and reported to the group that she went through a rough time at the end, but is now in 'a better place.' Her two cats are with her, and she "has asked to help our group." Stacie said her farewell, followed by someone who passed away many years ago—my Uncle Ray. He called out his name, with the familiar laughing lilt in his voice. He wanted Allyson and I to know that Mike, our cousin, also was with him. His voice then took a more serious note. He talked about our Dad, who is still living, faring badly. I asked him to send our greetings to everyone over on the other side. He said, "Yes he would do that, and our mother also extended her greetings back to Allyson and me." Daisy then told Uncle Ray to tell us that the circle was fading quickly. He said goodbye; a long silence and deep sigh ensued before we heard Allyson speak in her natural voice. Allyson said after a few moments that she knew that something unusual had happened. We said yes, this was wonderful with all the different spirits coming through! Before quitting the circle, Allyson heard the name 'Turner,' hoping someone in the group would recognize the name. When no one recognized it, Allyson listened further, adding, "I think this is not a relative, I believe 'Turner' is an artist. He shows me he was a landscape artist. He wants to help us with our card-precipitation sitting. I see he has about three surnames before the last name 'Turner,' I just cannot get any one of those." Just as we were about to turn up the red light, Allyson exclaimed, "William, one of the names is William! We will have to 'google' it on the internet, to see if we come up with a 'William Turner.'"

The red light followed by the white light made us eager to look for William Turner. Ten minutes later, we were crowded around Allyson's computer, to find that there was indeed an artist by the name of Joseph Mallord William Turner, known as William Turner, who lived from 1775 to 1851. He was known as 'the painter of light.' We have included his picture here at the end of this chapter. We feel energized and confident in the knowledge that we have higher beings watching over our weekly circle, and look forward to our entertaining these entities for many months, if not years, to come.

> *As long as we feel any emotion about them, whether of love, grief, resentment, or fear, we are actively in touch with them; we are affecting them, and they are affecting us. We should strive by all means in our power to achieve right relations with those who have passed over, and the most effectual way of achieving right relations is to possess accurate knowledge of inter-life conditions.*

Dion Fortune

William Turner

Allyson—Psychic Sense Training

Adele and I have long felt that anyone can learn the 'psychic sense' by utilizing discipline, perseverance, and focus. An old axiom states, "Give a man a fish, and he will eat for a day; teach a man to fish and he will eat for the rest of his life." If it is in our power to create change, to help effect a spiral dynamic for many to develop this God-given gift or power, we should effect this change if it is in humankind's best interest. The Bible exhorts us to do so, in Proverbs 3:27, "Withhold not good from them to whom it is due, when it is in the power of thine hand to do it." All benefit from not just developing psychic abilities, spiritual development must develop alongside. Teaching virtues are building blocks in a foundation for the growth of *siddhas*, or powers as the East Indians call it.

When I met my Master Guide Barnabas at the age of sixteen, he clarified for me the need to get out of my own way, that is, leave behind my ego when counseling others and delivering messages to those who need succor. He drilled in me the need for *values*. 'Integrity' was the value he impressed upon me when he later told me that my future career was to be a teacher.

The virtue of charity, which is another way of defining the power of unconditional love, is perhaps the greatest lesson needed upon this planet today. The word 'love' I use here is meant 'the source of all things, not limited to a feeling-state or particular action. Love welcomes everything and is free of everything, a sympathetic vibration.' Is this not the largest reason we need to reincarnate time and again, so that we might learn to be charitable? Barnabas states that when we are charitable, God helps us during adversity, He protects us from our enemies, heals us of our sicknesses. God provides if we need provision, and He shows charity to those that are charitable. Barnabas explains that as we open up to allow God work through us to help others, then we enjoy helping others. This is a blessing upon all involved—the giver and the receiver, but it helps amplify all effort to have the right outlook. Such is the axiom, "The right attitude creates right altitude."

Hopefully God understands the principle that to help one person, all benefit from the effort. Spirit has stated many times that if you help one or many, God is involved in this giving, and also receives, as well.

I decided to go visit one of my students in Winchester, Virginia, to work with a group she gathered together for a platform message group. I had talked to Ally several weeks before on the telephone about how she sounded 'different' in her voice. Five years earlier, Ally was a 'train wreck;' yet now a new foundation was laid, and obviously imprinted in her voice.

Ally is one of several students I trained in psychic and mediumship work. When Adele and I first met her she looked drained, weary. To say that she was confused and abused by her present employer was an understatement. She looked to both of us for clarification and support of her plight. She told us that outside of the fact that she was facing possible firing or laying-off from her job, she needed to know if there was something physically wrong with her. Her major problem was stress. Throughout our reading of her, I got the strong impression that here was a woman of great strength, but she could not see it. I told her that she herself was very psychic, needed to work on her extreme emotional confusion, and center herself through meditation to get answers. It would be over four years before she could do this last part for herself.

Ally came with her boyfriend, Steve, to a platform message group several months later, hoping to hear from some relatives in spirit for help. Ally still appeared wan and stressed. Steve came along to 'protect' his girlfriend. I recall that Ally's father came through by name, along with some other folks, to tell her to file a lawsuit against her employer, and to do this very soon, or it might be too late! She didn't understand the urgency of needing to do this, and she came up to me afterwards to ask why. I remember shrugging, telling her that her father must know why, but that spirit doesn't always clue us in to the reason.

Steve received a message from a cousin on the other side, telling him that the house being built for Ally and her son would have unexpected changes in building specs, as spirit showed me blueprint changes. Steve told Ally later, that he did not believe this message, but he was to find out a week later that the house unfortunately had the second floor plans turned around and built. The contractor admitted fault, and Ally ended up not paying full price for their house!

I decided to take Ally on as a student, regardless of her emotional and financial difficulties. Recognizing a psychic gem, she met along with other students at my home once a month. No one went away without learning, listening, and practice. I would bring other clients to class to assess my students' psychic awareness; Ally proved to be one of the best.

I was to see Ally again early in 2001 at another group, where spirit adamantly advised her to find an employment lawyer, and file suit. Ally went ahead with the suit. Her manager illegally fired her for not accepting a different job, unaware that company lawyers did not want any change in her status within the company. The right hand didn't know what the left hand was doing. Talking to her several months later over the telephone, I advised her that I felt it would be in her better interests to go with another lawyer that she interviewed. It seemed that her first advocate wasn't pushing hard enough for a good settlement. Spirit advised her that she could ask for more, or go to court and win more than the lawyers of her company were offering. The Department of Labor was willing to go to bat for Ally, and the company recognized their guilt. Due to her stress and insecurity, Ally blindly accepted the pittance that her company gave her. Just a few months later, her company filed for bankruptcy. Where Ally settled for $25,000, she could have gained $250,000 or more.

The company Ally worked for was WorldCom—ending up paying billions of dollars in fines for irregular and fraudulent practices. Ally was unable to find employment again in her field—she was now blacklisted. It was several years before her life turned around. Poor Ally, she suffered hardship, pain and humiliation.

In offering all of herself up to God at her lowest point, did God give her much in return. Ally today acknowledges that all of life offers opportunity to learn. Her spiritual training is truly now beginning; she is meditating and praying almost every night. She recognizes she is participating with spirit, and success is dependent upon her willingness to learn. When I hung the telephone from our conversation, I was awed by the immense change from the weak, conflicted individual she used to be. *Becoming is the true adventure.*

In February of 2005, the day I was to visit Ally for her platform group, I had a small family group at my office. Lori brought her mother, Linda, stepfather Bert, and Aunt Clara Belle for the first time. Lori looked nervous; they arrived a half-hour early. Inviting them in, they sat in the reading room anxiously while I had calls to return. While dialing the first call, I heard several people in spirit say their names, *Mary, Robert, Henry.* Mentally I asked them to wait patiently until I could begin the group reading.

The names stated came through for each individual that afternoon, and as usual, larger perspectives were sown, and skepticism receded for two present.

I asked Clara Belle her name and birth date. Over top of her voice I heard 'Robert' call his name out loudly. "Clara Belle, a man named Robert is here? Was he your husband?" She nodded yes. I pointed my finger to my chest area. "He tells me this area affected him before his passing. This is correct?" Again, Clara Belle nodded yes, and said, "He had lung cancer." It struck me that Clara Belle was very sad, holding back emotion. Bob acknowledged that their son, Bob Jr., was being difficult, that it would take a wing and a prayer to set him right with God. Clara Belle acknowledged this as well, stating that her son hadn't spoken to her in over a year. She felt hopeless that reconciliation would ever occur. I told her that prayer was all that we could ask for, and soon the group left for home. What I didn't know at the time was that Robert wasn't finished just yet. He wanted more attention later that evening!

I sat down on Ally's couch minutes before her group assembled that same evening. Ally was taking phone calls from attendees coming and not coming. Debbie, a friend of Ally's, sat on the couch to my left. Sure enough, spirit decided to get our attention!

All of us were busy talking, when suddenly, an 'electrical wind' microburst rushed through the living room into the dining room, shifting from left to right. Debbie nearly collapsed; she stated that she felt an electrical surge move through her. Minutes later Debbie felt completely 'charged' from all that electricity. I was speaking to Ally on my right when the microburst occurred; all the lights went out in the room, even the numerous candles were snuffed out! But, about ten seconds later, the lights came on, and the candles relit! We looked in stupefaction at each other. Ally and I were used to physical phenomena from spirit, although Debbie was new to this. She didn't stop talking about this until well into the night. Ally got up to see what clocks were affected; her microwave clock was flashing, and well as her Bose stereo.

Debbie and I stayed overnight with Ally. We sat up in the living room pondering the night's events. Ally started feeling nauseous, and stated she had the feeling that someone named 'Bob' had a message. I grabbed some paper and pen to quickly write down what was relayed. Ally said, "I hear the name 'Marybelle,' no, it's not that . . . it's 'Claribelle.' Do either of you know that name?" I acknowledged that 'Claribelle' was a woman from my group earlier today! "Well, I think this 'Bob' is her husband—did he die from cancer?" I admitted yes, we were definitely on to something here. "I keep hearing there is pain and loss with Claribelle—it would be better to 'let it go, and let God. Bob must have been tall, with a head of hair." Ally laughed. "I think he must have been handsome; he says he was from 'blue blood.'" Ally shifted in her seat, listening to the air. "He says that the son—the child—is disconnected, has no heart. There was some addiction. He is not in good health—I think he was underweight. Something about 'smoking.' No conscience. If there is something he took, he no longer has it." Ally paused again, and said, "I think he wants her to pray to St. Jude—I don't know why. I hear the words 'chocolates,' and 'spaghetti.' They must mean something to his wife Claribelle." Ally sighed, getting up from the chair. "Find out if any of this means anything." I reassured her that I would do this, tucking the note into my handbag.

It wasn't until the next morning that I realized that the clock in my bedroom never 'flashed' from the electrical shortout. I saw it, but I couldn't figure out just why, until I left for home later that day, that the microburst only affected two rooms. Ally left a message on my telephone when I got back to Arnold admitting the same thing. We knew now that what we experienced was either due to Bob's energetic emergency to get through, or it was Ally's spirit guide, 'White Hawk,' swooping in for the platform session. In either case, Deb was much impressed with the whole evening. She called a few days later, stating that she has been sitting with Ally in meditation in the evenings, and felt a deep need to receive more spiritual instruction. I told her to continue working with Ally in meditation.

I called Lori, Clara Belle's grandniece. Clara Belle called me later, and was able to verify most of the message, with the exception of 'spaghetti' and the son being underweight. Instead, he was grossly overweight, and she was afraid that she would outlive him. I silently agreed; this was a great possibility. 'Blue blood' piqued my curiosity—I asked Clara Belle if Bob Sr. came from a special background. "Yes, Allyson, Bob's mother was full-blooded Cherokee." I asked her about the 'chocolates.' Clara Belle, in her reserved voice, stated, "Oh, Bob would get me chocolates for Valentine's Day, you know, that was yesterday!" I slapped my cheek lightly—I had completely forgotten about the holiday! Great warmth came over me that moment. Both of us were hushed for several seconds. "Clara Belle," I said, "I am so glad Bob came back with another message. It is very rare for this to happen." I proceeded to tell her about the microburst of electrical energy, like a wind. She was overcome with emotion, and I could tell she was holding it in. I averred that I would pray for Bob Jr., hoping for a miracle.

The real miracle to me, though, is Ally's choice to bloom and expand as a person. So many people, mostly women, come up to us after our audiences and groups, and want to know how they, too, can develop the 'psychic sense.' It *is* time that more people bloom and expand into psychic awareness, but *spiritual awareness* is the key. The key is through training, incorporating many of the key concepts that are old and ever new to eager minds. It is our wish to enlarge the training of the "Psychic Sense™ Seminars" to benefit not just a few people, but thousands of eager participants. As Daniel Dunglas Home once stated to the woman who was to be his wife, "I have a mission entrusted to me. It is a great and holy one." Adele and I take this to be our mission statement!

> *"I believe in my heart that this power is being spread more and more every day to draw us nearer to God. You ask if it makes us purer? My only answer is that we are but mortals, and as such liable to err; but it does teach that the pure in heart shall see God. It teaches us that (s)He is love, and that there is no death. To the aged it comes as a solace, when the storms of life are nearly over and rest cometh. To the young it speaks of the duty we owe to each other, and that as we sow so shall we reap. To all it teaches resignation. It comes to roll away clouds of error, and bring the bright morning of a never-ending day."*

> D. D. Home, in a lecture given in London February 15, 1866.

To inquire about the Psychic Sense™ seminars, readings, audiences and other presentations with Allyson and Adele, Psy-dentical Twins, please go to *www.Psy-denticalTwins.com* or *www.Psy-Twins.com* for more information. You are welcome to call the office or email for appointments and other inquiries.

You are welcome to send us your personal stories of experiences with those on the other side, especially if it involves physical phenomena. We invite your participation, and may include your experience in a future book.

Allyson Walsh and Adele Nichols

Allyson and Adele wish to thank our contributors for the use of their art, photos, and facilities. Those listed below are available to contact:

Emily Grace Freed, Spirit Photographer
caffineoverdose@hotmail.com

Allen Gross, Spirit Photographer
Available for lectures and photography
(540) 420-1652
Ghosthunter1863@yahoo.com

Barbara Meneghini, Spirit Photographer
Trainsnow2000@yahoo.com

Barbara Roberts, Spirit Photographer
Barbara.Roberts.5555@gmail.com

Steve and Tina McNaughton
Chestnut Hall Bed and Breakfast
104 Lincoln Way West
New Oxford, PA 17350
(717) 624-8988
1-(888) 886-5660 toll-free
www.chestnuthallbb.com
chestnuthallbb@yahoo.com

Paranormal and Environmental Explanations from Research (P.E.E.R.)
www.peergb.com
hunters@peergb.com

Reverend Hoyt Robinette
is located at Camp Chesterfield,
which is also known as the Indiana Association of Spiritualists
50 Lincoln Drive * P.O. Box132
Chesterfield, Indiana 46017

Edwards Brothers Malloy
Thorofare, NJ USA
February 13, 2014